Eating Disorders

W9-AOH-721

Félix E. F. Larocca, *Editor*
BASH Treatment and Research Center

NEW DIRECTIONS FOR MENTAL HEALTH SERVICES
H. RICHARD LAMB, *Editor-in-Chief*
University of Southern California

Number 31, Fall 1986

Paperback sourcebooks in
The Jossey-Bass Social and Behavioral Sciences Series

Jossey-Bass Inc., Publishers
San Francisco • London

Félix E. F. Larocca (ed.).
Eating Disorders.
New Directions for Mental Health Services, no. 31.
San Francisco: Jossey-Bass, 1986.

New Directions for Mental Health Services
H. Richard Lamb, *Editor-in-Chief*

New Directions for Mental Health Services (publication number
USPS 493-910) is published quarterly by Jossey-Bass Inc., Publishers.
Second class postage paid at San Francisco, California, and at
additional mailing offices. POSTMASTER: Send address changes to
Jossey-Bass Inc., Publishers, 433 California Street, San Francisco,
California 94104.

Editorial correspondence should be sent to the Editor-in-Chief,
H. Richard Lamb, Department of Psychiatry and the Behavioral
Sciences, U.S.C. School of Medicine, 1934 Hospital Place,
Los Angeles, California 90033.

Library of Congress Catalog Card Number 85-81895

International Standard Serial Number ISSN 0193-9416

International Standard Book Number ISBN 1-55542-988-2

Cover art by WILLI BAUM

Manufactured in the United States of America

Ordering Information

The paperback sourcebooks listed below are published quarterly and can be ordered either by subscription or single-copy.

Subscriptions cost $40.00 per year for institutions, agencies, and libraries. Individuals can subscribe at the special rate of $30.00 per year *if payment is by personal check.* (Note that the full rate of $40.00 applies if payment is by institutional check, even if the subscription is designated for an individual.) Standing orders are accepted.

Single copies are available at $9.95 when payment accompanies order, and *all single-copy orders under $25.00 must include payment.* (California, New Jersey, New York, and Washington, D.C., residents please include appropriate sales tax.) For billed orders, cost per copy is $9.95 plus postage and handling. (Prices subject to change without notice.)

Bulk orders (ten or more copies) of any individual sourcebook are available at the following discounted prices: 10–49 copies, $8.95 each; 50–100 copies, $7.96 each; over 100 copies, *inquire.* Sales tax and postage and handling charges apply as for single copy orders.

Please note that these prices are for the academic year 1986–1987 and are subject to change without prior notice. Also, some titles may be out of print and therefore not available for sale.

To ensure correct and prompt delivery, all orders must give either the *name of an individual* or an *official purchase order number.* Please submit your order as follows:

Subscriptions: specify series and year subscription is to begin.
Single Copies: specify sourcebook code (such as, MHS1) and first two words of title.

Mail orders for United States and Possessions, Latin America, Canada, Japan, Australia, and New Zealand to:
Jossey-Bass Inc., Publishers
433 California Street
San Francisco, California 94104

Mail orders for all other parts of the world to:
Jossey-Bass Limited
28 Banner Street
London EC1Y 8QE

New Directions for Mental Health Services Series
H. Richard Lamb, *Editor-in-Chief*

MHS1   *Alternatives to Acute Hospitalization,* H. Richard Lamb
MHS2   *Community Support Systems for the Long-Term Patient,* Leonard I. Stein
MHS3   *Mental Health Consultations in Community Settings,*
Alexander S. Rogawski

Contents

Editor's Notes

Following the untimely death of Karen Carpenter and the subsequent admission by many television and radio personalities that they had suffered from eating disorders (Anorexia Nervosa and bulimia), universal interest and concern about eating disorders have suddenly proliferated. To date, numerous self-help organizations have been formed, journals have been devoted entirely to the understanding and treatment of these conditions, and a surplus of treatment centers for these conditions has been established in rapid profusion.

The medical profession has been bombarded from every conceivable angle by information and misinformation about these problems. To complicate matters, there is yet no systematic agreement on issues of nosology, psychopathology, or treatment. Treatment philosophies range from the entirely psychotherapeutic approach through the gamut of behaviorist approaches to those that utilize an addictive philosophy as a principle for treatment, failing to yield any consensus.

The field has further been obscured by the raising of questions as to whether Anorexia Nervosa and bulimia are part of the same continuum, whether they should be treated at units designated for this purpose alone, and as to whether obesity should be included in any treatment program, with eating disorders integrated.

In 1981, I founded a self-help organization in St. Louis, BASH, which has proved to be instrumental in the formation of a treatment program for patients with eating disorders. This would operate in tandem with the work of a self-help organization and a hospital unit dedicated to this purpose.

This approach necessitated a revision, and in 1985 BASH became Behavior Adaption Support and Healing, in addition to its original Bulimia Anorexia Self-Help purpose. This evolutionary move was mandated by the need to provide our patients with greater latitude in treatment options, de-emphasizing the isolation and segregation of eating-disorders patients by diagnostic category alone.

This volume of *New Directions for Mental Health Services* addresses some of the most important issues currently evolving in the field of eating disorders and how they may relate to mood disorders.

Chapter One, on understanding medical complications, provides a

This volume would not have been possible without the assistance of Sandy Blue, R.N., Larry Fiquette, Annette R. Walker, Audrey M. Holweg, and, most of all, my research assistant, Sherry Goodner, R.N.

1

historical introduction to the eating-disorders field, with a progression into the many deleterious complications of these diseases as they affect their victims. This chapter has in it the vigor of combining a discussion of the effects of semi-starvation with related concerns of interest to the clinician. Its clear exposition makes it of particular interest to mental health professionals, who need to know about medical as well as psychological issues in these disorders.

Chapter Two once again addresses the possibility that Anorexia Nervosa is a variant of an affective and mood disorder. Bulimia Nervosa, which can be construed as an extension of the Anorexia Nervosa syndrome and as an entity by itself, is considered not only as a distant variant of a mood disorder but also as amenable to treatment utilizing the same methodology for formal affective and mood disorders (see also Pope and Hudson's chapter, this volume). Rodrigo A. Muñoz and Henry Amado support for research into the investigation of the relationship between anorexia, as an eating disorder, and its possible concomitant mood disorder.

Chapter Three gives the reader a rather sobering and parsimonious review of the role of the nutritionist in the treatment of eating disorders. Johanna T. Dwyer, whose writings are of much interest to those concerned about the safety of some diets, and whose contributions to the field of eating disorders are numerous, once again gives her warnings and caveats to dietitians who have found in their training and background sufficient knowledge to become self-appointed therapists in the management of patients suffering from eating disorders. A distinction between solo practice and performance is made, to complement the findings in Chapter Nine that nutritional advice by itself in most cases is unwise.

Chapter Four is a most important and relevant section of this sourcebook, since eating disorders are commonly thought to be either Anorexia Nervosa or bulimia nervosa, but scant attention is paid to such conditions as coprophagia, rumination, and other disturbances, such as pica. These and other conditions are no rarities and may open a new door to the advancement of knowledge—not to compartmentalize anorexia and bulimia, but to re-establish these conditions in the mainstream of the continuum of the eating-disorder pathological sequence.

Chapter Five, "Males With Eating Disorders," is included because this underdiagnosed condition tends to baffle practitioners who are neither prepared to find nor trained to investigate this not-so-rare association. Eating disorders in males seem to be appearing with greater frequency; in our eating- and mood-disorders program, we have found this association to be a growing phenomenon.

Chapter Six is on the pathogenesis and treatment of obesity. It has become customary for some authors to exclude obesity from the spectrum of normal dieting, anorexia, and bulimia, and also to downplay restrained eating (normal dieting), thus leaving the main stage to Anorexia Nervosa and bulimia nervosa. This chapter provides exhaustive and authoritative information for the interested reader.

Chapter Seven underscores the growing relevance of neuropharmacology, providing an "embarras de richesses" to the treatment of these conditions. This chapter and Chapter Eight review current studies and complement each other while leaving room for the authors of Chapter Eight to review such issues as psychotherapeutic efforts, group psychotherapy, and self-help. These chapters provide an update on all treatment philosophies to date.

Chapter Nine is on tube feeding, an ever-necessary issue. (Vandereycken and Meermann, 1984, mention it, along with the reservations some may have about tube feeding as a therapeutic tool in the treatment of restrictive Anorexia Nervosa.) The authors provide, with appropriate theoretical formulations, a classic example of how tube feeding can be administered and of how it was viewed by a patient who kept a diary while receiving this form of care. If this chapter does not settle the controversy about this therapeutic approach, at least it will shed some light on the usefulness of tube feeding for selected patients.

Chapter Ten presents a review of the formulations and applications of ego psychology in this field. This chapter constitutes a source of information for therapists whose training and background consist primarily of psychodynamic formulations and who are interested in finding a source of eclecticism.

Finally, Chapter Eleven gives the reader advice on technique and methodology in the use of hypnosis for the treatment of eating disorders.

At a time when financial resources are dwindling under the impact of consumer groups and the hospital industry, a volume that contributes a down-to-earth, systematic review of the state of the art would seem a necessity. This volume, although thorough, cannot be exhaustive, as this field is in a state of flux and rapid progression. It does not provide a list of self-help organizations, which can be found in almost every professional and nonprofessional publication. Instead, it furnishes the reader with sound, up-to-date knowledge.

Félix E. F. Larocca
Editor

Reference

Vandereycken, W., and Meermann, R. *Anorexia Nervosa: A Clinician's Guide to Treatment.* New York: Walter de Gruyter, 1984.

Félix E. F. Larocca, M.D., is medical director of BASH Treatment and Research Center for Eating and Mood Disorders in St. Louis, Missouri. He is also president and founder of BASH (Bulimia Anorexia Self-Help/Behavior Adaption Support and Healing), Inc.

The medical complications of eating disorders can be so varied and subtle that one must always be alert.

Understanding Medical Complications of Eating Disorders

George W. Bo-Linn

Eating disorders can be defined as disturbances in eating behavior that result in injury to a person's physical or psychological health.

Anorexia Nervosa was first defined almost three hundred years ago by Richard Morton, when he described a seventeen-year-old girl who was "like a skeleton only clad with skin" (Lucas, 1981). Although Sir William Gull and Charles Laségue, a French contemporary, both described additional patients in more clinical detail, Gull (1874) coined the term *Anorexia Nervosa.*

Actually, Anorexia Nervosa is a misnomer, since such patients have no loss of appetite, but rather are morbidly preoccupied with food. Similarly, bulimia, which means "ox hunger," is a misnomer, as regards this kind of patient. While these patients binge-eat enormous numbers of calories, they are not hungry, and they carefully plan their binges. Bulimic anorectic patients, as the name implies, reveal characteristics of both anorexia and bulimia. They combine binge eating with postprandial purging, accomplished by self-induced emesis and abuse of cathartic and diuretic drugs.

The true prevalence of eating disorders is not known. However,

F.E.F. Larocca (ed.). *Eating Disorders.*
New Directions for Mental Health Services, no. 31. San Francisco: Jossey-Bass, Fall 1986.

5

estimates range from 1 percent (Crisp and others, 1976) to 50 percent of adolescent women, and 10 percent of college-age men (Harris, 1983). Exact estimates are difficult because of varying definitions; the covertness of patients, who do not wish to arouse suspicion of their eating behavior; and the subclinical form of the disease.

It is precisely because of the subterfuge practiced by patients that health professionals must be cognizant of the varied and subtle complications of eating disorders. The classic description of a patient with anorexia is of a young woman who has starved herself to the point that she indeed looks "like a skeleton clad only in skin." More often, however, one finds a person who, while not fat, is not emaciated. Patients with bulimia are usually of normal weight. Nevertheless, the complications of eating disorders usually can be explained either by the restriction of calories or by purging to rid oneself of ingested calories.

Symptoms and Physical Findings

The medical complications of Anorexia Nervosa are generally those of starvation. The symptoms and physical findings bring to mind the cachectic survivors of prisoner-of-war camps. While patients with anorexia tend to minimize their symptoms, they will usually have amenorrhea (Warren and VandeWeile, 1975); sleep disturbances (Crisp and others, 1980); cold intolerance, often accompanied by cyanosis and numbness of the extremities (Halmi, 1978); and skin changes, such as hairiness and scaliness (Silverman, 1977).

The physical examination of patients with classic anorexia is notable for general effects of starvation. The body responds to this cachexia by a slowing of the heart (bradycardia) and a lowering of the blood pressure (hypotension). Peripheral edema is present, as seen in other disorders related to starvation. In anorexia, however, the edema is thought to be due to failure to mobilize fluid from the legs, rather than to low protein intake (resulting in hypoalbuminia). Of some diagnostic usefulness is the faintly yellow cast to the skin, due to carotenemia, not present in patients with other forms of semi-starvation.

Despite the similarities between starved individuals and patients with Anorexia Nervosa, there are notable differences. Since anorectic patients have self-induced starvation, they often "select" certain food categories to avoid and therefore usually do not develop frank vitamin deficiency. The maintained muscle strength and energy levels are surprising, and the reasons are unclear.

There is no diagnostic guidelines of physical signs and laboratory findings in patients with eating disorders. Hence, one must rely on diagnostic criteria that include both psychological and physical changes. The laboratory profile, however, is helpful in that findings that are not generally associated with eating disorders, such as an elevated erythrocyte sedimentation rate or white blood cell count, should make the physician suspicious that another diagnosis should be considered.

In contrast to patients with classic anorexia, bulimic patients are usually distressed by their eating disorder and are less apt to hide or deny their problems and symptoms. Furthermore, the bulimic is usually of normal weight, achieved by rigid adherence to binge-purge behavior. Hence, the complications of bulimia more often result from bingeing, followed by purging with laxatives and diuretics, rather than from self-imposed starvation. Thus, symptoms of bulimia are less observable, as compared to those of anorexia. For example, normal menses are usually present and are probably a reflection of the patient's normal weight. Depression is often a complaint, as are episodes of impulsive behavior, such as alcohol and drug abuse. Symptoms of substance abuse in a female adolescent may trigger suspicion of bulimia.

As for the physical examination, bulimics are usually not cachectic and do not exhibit the physical findings described in anorectic patients. There may be, however, stigmata of drug abuse or episodes of self-mutilation.

Laboratory Findings

Just as the physical findings reflect the degree of starvation (Anorexia Nervosa) or binge-purge behavior (bulimia), so do the laboratory findings. Hence, neither anorectic nor bulimic patients have "diagnostic" laboratory abnormalities. Severe malnutrition, whatever the cause, can result in anemia, low white cell and platelet numbers, and relative lymphocytosis. Two laboratory abnormalities of interest are elevated beta-carotene levels (Schwabe and others, 1981) and high cholesterol levels in the blood (Mordasini and others, 1978). There is no ready explanation for either finding.

Gastrointestinal: Esophageal. Esophageal complications can occur because of the mechanical and chemical injury to the esophagus from repeated vomiting. These complications include esophagitis, Mallory-Weiss tears, and rupture. Gastric acid, as it bathes the esophageal mucosa during vomiting, can cause esophagitis severe enough to result in stricture formation. Retching places tremendous stress on the esophagus, with rapid rises in esophageal pressures as high as 300mm/Hg, and can cause rents in the lining known as Mallory-Weiss tears (Mallory and Weiss, 1929). These tears can bleed massively. Perforation, or rupture of the esophagus, can also result from vigorous vomiting. This injury occurs at the lower end of the esophagus, too. While a Mallory-Weiss tear generally stops bleeding and usually does not require surgical repair, an esophageal rupture is catastrophic and life-threatening. Immediate surgery is necessary.

Gastrointestinal: Gastric and Intestinal. Gastric complications of eating disorders include gastritis, decreased acid secretion, delayed gastric emptying, acute gastric dilatation, and rupture. Total acid secretion in the stomach has been described as significantly less in patients with anorexia than in normal subjects. This decrease persists even after patients gain weight (DuBois and others, 1979).

Delayed gastric emptying also occurs and may contribute to postprandial discomfort, fullness, and the abdominal pain noted by some anorectic patients. The mechanism of the impaired emptying is unknown, although administering bethanechol, a parasympathomimetic agent, will temporarily increase gastric emptying in these patients (DuBois and others, 1981).

Acute gastric dilatation is an uncommon but well-described complication. A combination of factors plays a role, but dilatation may be due in part to rapid ingestion of large meals in combination with delayed gastric emptying. Should dilatation be so severe that the pressure within the stomach exceeds the pressure within the veins, then tissue death can occur. Gastric rupture, another life-threatening complication, can then result. Other common gastrointestinal complications include the superior-mesenteric artery syndrome (SMAS) and generalized ileus.

Colonic complications commonly occur from laxative abuse. Laxatives, although ineffective in significantly reducing calorie absorption, are often used in enormous quantities (Bo-Linn and others, 1983).

Cardiovascular. Patients with eating disorders may have impaired cardiovascular function, with decreased blood pressure and reduced cardiac output and heart rate. The heart is abnormal, with thinning of the pumping chambers and reduction of chamber size (Fohlin, 1977). Presumably these changes are in response to malnutrition. Many electrocardiographic changes have been reported. Electrolyte abnormalities cause many of the cardiac arrhythmias. Intrinsic conduction defects have been found, however, and sudden deaths occur as a result of hypokalemia (loss of potassium). Ipecac abuse has been linked to several deaths of patients with eating disorders. The active ingredient of ipecac syrup, emetine, has marked cardiomyotoxicity.

Pulmonary. Because of self-induced vomiting, the anorectic or bulimic patient risks aspiration pneumonia and pneumomediastinum (Donley and Kemple, 1978).

Endocrine/Metabolic. It appears that the endocrine abnormalities that have been described in eating disorders are secondary to starvation, since there is no evidence for primary pituitary, gonadal, thyroid, or adrenal dysfunction. The abnormalities are related to malnutrition. Although the occurrence of an eating disorder in a patient with diabetes mellitus is relatively uncommon, inability to control the blood glucose should alert the physician to this possibility (Hillard and Hillard, 1984).

Amenorrhea and estrogen deficiency are the best understood of endocrine disturbances associated with anorexia (Warren and VandeWeile, 1975); approximately 20 percent of patients are known to develop amenorrhea prior to the onset of the illness. The primary defect resides in the hypothalamus. Release of gonadotropin-releasing hormone is impaired, resembling a prepubertal pattern (Boyar and others, 1974). With weight gain, some restoration of the normal pattern generally occurs, but in at least 25 percent of patients the amenorrhea persists.

In male anorectics, serum testosterone levels are low (McNab and Hawton, 1981), which may explain the impotence and low libido in these patients.

Other pituitary hormones have been found to be at abnormal levels in patients with anorexia. Growth hormone levels are often elevated, probably as a result of decreased somatomedin C levels (Frankel and Jenkins, 1975).

Vasopressin, another pituitary hormone, is depressed or erratic in patients with anorexia, as it is in individuals who have been starved (Gold and others, 1983).

Endocrine: Thyroid. Although anorectic patients have signs and symptoms suggestive of hypothyroidism, they do not have a true low-thyroid state (Moshang and Utiger, 1977). Under the stress of malnutrition, the metabolic activity of the thyroid is impaired, and elevated T4 and reverse T3 levels are often found in these patients.

Endocrine: Adrenal. Malnourished anorectics may have a shift in adrenal metabolism that results in altered levels of active androgens.

Mean plasma cortisol levels are normal or elevated in anorectic patients. Elevated levels may be secondary to decreased metabolism of cortisol (Boyar and Bradlow, 1977; Boyar and others, 1977) or to increased cortisol production (Walsh and others, 1981). In addition, dexamethasone suppression tests are abnormal.

Norepinephrine levels are low, as they are in any starved patients (Young and Landsberg, 1977).

Renal. Because of fluid and electrolyte depletion resulting from vomiting and purging, the bulimic patient is particularly at risk for life-threatening complications. Chronically dehydrated, and often with low potassium levels, the bulimic patient can develop kidney stones and renal insufficiency and even failure. The typical hypochloremic, hypokalemic metabolic alkalosis of chronic vomiting requires immediate identification and treatment.

Hematologic. Low white blood cell counts, decreased white blood cell function, low platelet counts, and mild anemia may occur in anorexia. The bone marrow is often hypocellular, with decreased fat content (Myers and others, 1981). The degree of abnormalities does not correlate with the amount or duration of weight loss. Immunocompetency is preserved in anorexia until weight loss is extremely severe. Seldom are these patients found to succumb to the bacterial infections that result in such symptoms as seen in a cold or the flu.

Musculoskeletal. Osteoporosis is an increasingly recognized complication of anorexia (Rigotti and others, 1984). Low calcium intake and estrogen deficiency probably account for the reduced bone mass.

Muscle abnormalities may be secondary to electrolyte depletion. Chronic ipecac syrup ingestion can also cause toxic peripheral muscle weakness and cardiac muscle weakness (Brotman and others, 1981).

Neurologic. Few neurologic complications have been described in the literature. Hypoglycemic and hyperglycemic comas are probably the most serious.

Peripheral nerve palsies can occur secondary to nerve compression from marked cachexia and loss of cushioning subcutaneous tissue (Schott, 1979). The peroneal nerve is particularly vulnerable.

Dermatologic. Patients with eating disorders, particularly those who self-induce vomiting and purging, may exhibit dermatologic complications. Phenolphthalein, an ingredient in most over-the-counter laxatives, can cause a drug reaction (Wyatt and others, 1972). These skin lesions recur at the same site upon repeated exposure to phenolphthalein and may develop brownish-gray hyperpigmentation over time. Subconjunctival hemorrhages of the blood vessels in the eye may result from excessive and forceful vomiting.

References

Bo-Linn, G. W., Santa Ana, C. A., Morawski, S. G., and Fordtran, J. S. "Purging and Calorie Absorption in Bulimic Patients and Normal Women." *Annals of Internal Medicine,* 1983, *99,* 14–26.

Boyar, R. M., and Bradlow, H. L. "Studies of Testosterone Metabolism in Anorexia Nervosa." In R. A. Vigersky (ed.), *Anorexia Nervosa.* New York: Raven Press, 1977.

Boyar, R. M., Hellman, L. D., Roffwarg, H., and Katz, J. "Cortisol Secretion and Metabolism in Anorexia Nervosa." *New England Journal of Medicine,* 1977, *296,* 190–193.

Boyar, R. M., Katz, J., Finkelstein, J. W., Kapen, S., Weiner, H., Weitzman, E. D., and Hellman, L. "Anorexia Nervosa: Immaturity of the 24-Hour Luteinizing Hormone Secretory Pattern." *New England Journal of Medicine,* 1974, *291,* 861–865.

Brotman, M. C., Forbath, N., Garfinkel, P. E., and Humphrey, J. "Myopathy Due to Ipecac Syrup Poisoning in a Patient with Anorexia Nervosa." *Canadian Medical Association Journal,* 1981, *125,* 453–454.

Crisp, A. H., Hsu, L.K.G., Harding, B., and Hartshorn, J. "Clinical Features of Anorexia Nervosa: A Study of a Consecutive Series of 102 Female Patients." *Journal of Psychosomatic Research,* 1980, *24,* 179–191.

Crisp, A. H., Palmer, R. L., and Kalucy, R. S. "How Common Is Anorexia Nervosa? A Prevalence Study." *British Journal of Psychiatry,* 1976, *128,* 549–554.

Donley, A. J., and Kemple, T. J. "Spontaneous Pneumomediastinum Complicating Anorexia Nervosa." *British Medical Journal*, 1978, *1*, 1604-1605.

DuBois, A., Gross, H. A., Ebert, M. H., and Castell, D. O. "Altered Gastric Emptying and Secretion in Primary Anorexia Nervosa." *Gastroenterology*, 1979, *77*, 319-323.

DuBois, A., Gross, H. A., Richter, J. E., and Ebert, M. H. "Effect of Bethanecol on Gastric Functions of Primary Anorexia Nervosa." *Digestive Diseases and Science*, 1981, *26*, 598-600.

Fohlin, L. "Body Composition, Cardiovascular and Renal Function in Adolescent Patients with Anorexia Nervosa." *Acta Paediatrica Scandanavica*, 1977, *268*, 1-78.

Frankel, R. J., and Jenkins, J. S. "Hypothalamic-Pituitary Function in Anorexia Nervosa." *Acta Endocrinology* (Copenhagen), 1975, *78*, 209-221.

Gold, P. W., Kaye, W., Robertson, G. L., and Ebert, M. H. "Abnormalities in Plasma and Cerebrospinal-Fluid Arginine Vasopressin in Patients with Anorexia Nervosa." *New England Journal of Medicine*, 1983, *308*, 1117-1123.

Gull, W. W. "Anorexia Nervosa (Apepsia Hysterica, Anorexia Hysterica)." *Transactions of the Clinical Society of Medicine*, 1874, *7*, 22-28.

Halmi, K. A. "Anorexia Nervosa: Recent Investigations." *Annual Medicine*, 1978, *29*, 137-148.

Harris, R. T. "Bulimarexia and Related Serious Eating Disorders with Medical Complications." *Annals of Internal Medicine*, 1983, *99*, 800-807.

Hillard, J. R., and Hillard, P.J.A. "Bulimia, Anorexia Nervosa, and Diabetes: Deadly Combinations." *Psychiatric Clinics of North America*, 1984, *7*, 367-379.

Lucas, A. R. "Toward the Understanding of Anorexia Nervosa as a Disease Entity." *Mayo Clinic Proceedings*, 1981, *56*, 254-264.

McNab, D., and Hawton, K. "Disturbance of Sex Hormones in Anorexia Nervosa in the Male." *Postgraduate Medical Journal*, 1981, *57*, 254-256.

Mallory, G. K., and Weiss, S. "Hemorrhages from Lacerations of the Cardiac Orifice of the Stomach Due to Vomiting." *American Journal of Medical Science*, 1929, *178*, 506-510.

Mordasini, R., Klose, G., and Greten, H. "Secondary Type II Hyperlipoproteinemia in Patients with Anorexia Nervosa." *Metabolism*, 1978, *27*, 71-79.

Moshang, T., Jr., and Utiger, R. D. "Low Triiodothyronine Euthyroidism in Anorexia Nervosa." In R. A. Vigersky (ed.), *Anorexia Nervosa*. New York: Raven Press, 1977.

Myers, T. J., Perkerson, M. D., Witter, B. A., and Granville, N. B. "Hematologic Findings in Anorexia Nervosa." *Connecticut Medicine*, 1981, *45*, 14-17.

Rigotti, N. A., Nussbaum, S. R., Herzog, D. B., and Neer, R. M. "Osteoporosis in Women with Anorexia Nervosa." *New England Journal of Medicine*, 1984, *311*, 1601-1606.

Schott, G. D. "Anorexia Nervosa Presenting as Foot Drop." *Postgraduate Medical Journal*, 1979, *55*, 58-60.

Schwabe, A. D., Lippe, B. M., Chang, R. J., Pops, M. A., and Yager, J. "Anorexia Nervosa." *Annals of Internal Medicine*, 1981, *94*, 371-381.

Silverman, J. A. "Anorexia Nervosa: Clinical and Metabolic Observations in a Successful Treatment Plan." In R. A. Vigersky (ed.), *Anorexia Nervosa*. New York: Raven Press, 1977.

Walsh, B. T., Katz, J. L., Levin, J., Kream, J., Fukushimo, D. K., Weiner, H., and Zumoff, B. "The Production Rate of Cortisol Declines During Recovery from Anorexia Nervosa." *Journal of Clinical Endocrinology and Metabolism*, 1981, *53*, 203-205.

Warren, M. P., and VandeWeile, R. L. "Clinical and Metabolic Features of Anorexia Nervosa." *American Journal of Obstetrics and Gynecology*, 1975, *117*, 435–439.

Wyatt, E., Greaves, M., and Sondergaard, J. "Fixed Drug Eruption (Phenolphtalein): Evidence for a Blood-Borne Mediator." *Archives of Dermatology*, 1972, *106*, 671–673.

Young, J. B., and Landsberg, L. "Suppression of Sympathetic Nervous System During Fasting." *Science*, 1977, *196*, 1473–1475.

George W. Bo-Linn is associate gastroenterologist at St. John's Mercy Medical Center in St. Louis, Missouri.

Attempting to define Anorexia Nervosa among psychiatric disorders reveals many similarities to affective disorders, but several major discrepencies remain.

Anorexia Nervosa: An Affective Disorder

Rodrigo A. Muñoz, Henry Amado

Because psychiatric disorders are manifested as a confusing array of clinical pictures at different times in their natural course, Robins and Guze (1970) have proposed five phases of investigation for establishing diagnostic validity over time for certain illnesses. This is thought to be especially useful in the absence of diagnostically accurate laboratory tests in psychiatry. The five phases are clinical description, laboratory studies, delimitation from other disorders (differential diagnosis to exclude other illnesses), follow-up studies, and family studies. An application of the five phases to our current knowledge about Anorexia Nervosa led us to think of this disorder as associated with affective disorders.

The clinical picture of Anorexia Nervosa may include feelings of sadness, ideas of suicide, and suicidal behavior. Although most patients with anorexia do not meet the diagnostic criteria for major affective disorder, the overall picture may be more typical of affective disorder than of classical anorexia, as was the case with the following patients.

Patient 1

This was a twenty-two-year-old single female who was being treated by her family physician for severe depression. Her history indicated that she

F.E.F. Larocca (ed.). *Eating Disorders.*
New Directions for Mental Health Services, no. 31. San Francisco: Jossey-Bass, Fall 1986.

had "always been depressed" and that she could remember being depressed even when she entered grammar school. Her depression had usually been accompanied by fluctuations in weight, lack of sleep, difficulty in thinking and concentrating, feelings of guilt, and a desire to die. The patient said that on several occasions she had thought of killing herself.

The patient had had a subclinical depression for at least two years. During this time, she had had many ups and downs, periods of well-being alternating with sadness and discouragement, and feelings of guilt.

She was admitted to the hospital for observation because of failure to respond to tricyclic antidepressants and supportive psychotherapy.

Observation in the hospital led to a diagnosis of anorexia after the staff became more aware of her intense preoccupation with weight, food, and exercise, as well as her persistent denial that she was eating much less than she should. Further inquiry revealed that she had lost a large amount of weight—as much as 20.5 kg two years prior to her admission—and had kept her weight down by eating poorly and exercising strenuously every day. Her family was known to the hospital because both her parents and her sister had been treated for severe depression.

Patient 2

She was a fifty-nine-year-old businesswoman, a divorced mother of three, who was admitted because of despondency, pessimism, and discouragement.

She gave a history of several episodes of depression (starting in her twenties), each of which lasted between eighteen months and two years. She had undergone intensive psychotherapy and had had long periods of good adjustment. She seemed to suffer a typical unipolar affective disorder.

It took several interviews with the patient's husband and her two daughters to uncover a history of her persistent desire to be thin, accompanied by careful planning of meals, daily jogging of at least ten miles, and persistent use of laxatives. Even though the patient looked thin when she came to the hospital, she insisted that she was actually quite fat and in need of control to prevent obesity. The family revealed that the emphasis on thinness and minimal weight had been present even when she was not depressed and had preceded the onset of the first bout of depression.

No specific laboratory findings for anorexia exist. Those that have been used do not differentiate between anorexia and mood disorders. Thyroid tests, studies of cortisol levels, and other evaluations of possible biological markers have been found inconclusive in both disorders.

Follow-up studies suggest a relationship between anorexia and affective disorders. In Theander's (1970) study, twenty-seven out of ninety-four anorectics were depressed at follow-up. Three additional patients had committed suicide. Among Morgan and Russell's (1978) forty-one patients, 45 percent were depressed at follow-up. Cantwell and others (1977) interviewed eighteen former anorectics and gave diagnoses of seven "definite" and one "probable" affective disorders. We have seen several patients with a history of anorexia accompanied by depression.

Patient 3

This thirty-seven-year-old married female, mother of three, an interior decorator, had received psychiatric treatment fifteen years prior to her recent clinic visit. Her initial hospital admission occurred when she was eighteen years old. At that time, she had tried for four years to keep a minimal weight. She had gone from 63.7 kg to about 44.0 kg. She had suffered Anorexia Nervosa for most of the time, had developed lanugo (downy body hair), had an emaciated appearance, and was worried that she was still too fat. She was given a diagnosis of anorexia and treated in a program of behavior modification that included the use of a nasogastric tube and regular feedings according to her weight fluctuations. She improved and left the hospital at a time when she weighed 57.7 kg. She was eating three normal meals a day and had returned to work. She was then free of symptoms for fourteen years.

The current picture, which lasted six months, was one of severe depression with sadness, pessimism, discouragement, loss of sleep, difficulty in thinking and concentrating, inability to make decisions, and thoughts of suicide. During this episode, she did not lose weight, even though she complained about lack of appetite. She met the criteria for major depressive disorder but did not have the symptoms that characterized her initial period of anorexia.

Family Studies

Of the twenty-six anorectics studied by Cantwell, two fathers, fifteen mothers, and six siblings were diagnosed as having an affective disorder. When Winokur and others (1980) compared twenty-five anorectics and twenty-five normal controls, the relatives of those with anorexia had a 22 percent incidence of affective disorder, whereas only 10 percent of the relatives of controls had such histories.

New evidence has appeared indicating an association between Anorexia Nervosa and affective disorders. The case histories below represent follow-up studies, family studies, twin studies, and studies of suicide reported since 1983.

Follow-up Studies

Steinhausen and Glanville (1983) have made a systematic analysis of the available literature. Depressive symptoms or personality traits were present in between 3 percent and 87 percent, with an average of 31 percent of anorectics participating in follow-up studies. The findings were unreliable because the duration of follow-up varied from one to fifty years, although in most studies depressive symptoms were recorded with moderate frequency.

Searching for more systematic and precise information, one finds the study by Tolstrup and others (1985), with indications that out of 151 patients who were re-examined anywhere from four to twenty-two years (averaging twelve-and-a-half years) after first contact, 6 had commited suicide, 15 suffered "neurosis," 9 suffered psychotic depression, and 7 suffered other psychoses. Only 61, or 47 percent, were free of mental disorder. The results suggested that at follow-up, a large portion suffered disorders associated with affective disorders.

Family Studies

Rivinus and others (1984) analyzed the family histories of forty young women with anorexia and twenty-three control women of similar age. There was more evidence of depression and substance-use disorders among close relatives of the anorectics. Their pedigrees differed significantly from those of the controls in a higher frequency of depression and substance-use disorders in consecutive generations (and in the family "loading" for these disorders). The results of this study suggest an association between anorexia and familial risk for affective and related disorders.

Gershon and others (1984) studied twenty-four unrelated anorectic probands who had been admitted for treatment to the inpatient program of NIMH or to the Phipps Clinic of Johns Hopkins Hospital. Their relatives had a prevalence of affective disorders similar to that found among the relatives of patients suffering affective disorder.

In our practice, we often had patients who were the only ones in their families suffering anorexia, but there were several relatives who had clear histories of depression. That was the case with Patient 1 and with Patient 4.

Patient 4

This seventeen-year-old female high school student, brought in by her parents, suffered typical manifestations of anorexia—a 25 percent weight loss, refusal to eat, excessive exercising, persistent weighing of herself, insistence that she was overweight, intense concern about dieting and food, and denial that she had any problem.

The family history was positive for an affective disorder in that the mother had received ECT (electroconvulsive treatment, or shock treatment) after she had been depressed and attempted suicide at the age of thirty-seven. The maternal grandfather had killed himself after several treatments for depression. None of the relatives in the paternal or maternal lines had a history of anorexia. A sister, twenty-one, was reported to have abused alcohol, to have run away from home, and to have experimented with drugs. This sister had undergone therapy and was free of problems when we took the patient's history.

Suicide Studies

Studies of suicide among patients with anorexia are important, not only because follow-up studies generally indicate that a significant number have killed themselves but also because suicidal behavior may be a clue to the association between anorexia and depression.

Viesselman and Roig (1985) studied this problem. In their group of thirteen anorectics, eleven (85 percent) suffered depression, 75 percent had made impulsive suicide attempts, and 66 percent had made serious attempts. These figures concerning anorectics who attempt or commit suicide are remarkably similar to corresponding data for patients with primary affective disorder.

Twin Studies

As pointed out by Hsu and others (1984), there have been several shortcomings in reports about anorectics who were identical twins. The follow-up periods were short, the twins had separated, the nonaffected twins have not been fully studied, and some criteria have been inadequately defined. They reported on a set of identical twins, both suffering from an affective disorder, but only one whom had been previously anorectic. They proposed that families with affective disorders predispose (presumably through genetics and environment) the development of anorexia in adolescent females at a time in their lives when maturation, separation, and identity issues are important.

Discussion

The application of these investigative guidelines, initially put forth by Robins and Guze to identify psychiatric disorders, suggests an overlap of anorexia and affective disorder in many caes, although not in all. Finding evidence of such an association over time and across a great diversity of clinical presentations is difficult, but those interested in studying the relationship between affective disorder and anorexia have received support from an increasing number of studies in recent years. The suggestion of an association between the two clinical entities seems too strong to ignore, particularly in view of the therapeutic implications. Perhaps a substantial subgroup of individuals afflicted with anorexia would respond best to treatment designed as though they suffered from an affective disorder.

Critics of this notion point out, correctly, that a premature conclusion that Anorexia Nervosa is a form of "atypical" affective disorder would obscure important discrepancies. For example, Altshuler and Weiner (1985) note that the two disorders seem to differ greatly in a number of demographic parameters:

1. Major depressive disorders have a female-to-male ratio of two to one, but anorexia has a female-to-male ratio much more disproportionate, ranging between seven to one and twenty to one.

2. Affective disorders seem to be equally distributed throughout the socioeconomic spectrum, but anorexia has usually been said to have a predilection for the upper classes.

3. Affective disorders seem to involve persons with a broad range of intelligence, while anorexia has a clear predilection for intelligent women.

Further research on the diagnostic classification of Anorexia Nervosa may be anticipated in years to come. Following the trend of current findings, we expect that a closer relationship will be found with affective disorders than with other psychiatric entities, such as schizophrenia and organic brain syndromes.

It may develop that patients meeting criteria for both affective disorder and anorexia constitute a distinct, nonrandom population that would differ from a corresponding group of anorectics without apparent affective disorder. Comparisons between patients suffering from affective disorder and their counterparts of the same age, sex, social class, and intellect suffering from anorexia will produce a better understanding of the current difficulties.

References

Altshuler, K. Z., and Weiner, M. F. "Anorexia Nervosa and Depression: A Dissenting View." *American Journal of Psychiatry*, 1985, *142* (3), 328–332.

Cantwell, D. P., Sturzenberger, S., Burroughs, J., Salkin, B., and Green, J. K. "Anorexia Nervosa: An Affective Disorder?" *Archives of General Psychiatry*, 1977, *34*, 1087–1093.

Gershon, E. S., Schreiber, J. L., Hamovit, J. R., Dibble, E. D., Kaye, W., Nurnberger, J. I., Andersen, A. E., and Ebert, M. H. "Clinical Findings on Patients with Anorexia Nervosa and Affective Illness in Their Relatives." *American Journal of Psychiatry*, 1984, *141*, 1419–1422.

Hsu, L.K.G., Holder, D., Hindmarsh, D., and Phelps, C. "Bipolar Illness Preceded by Anorexia Nervosa in Identical Twins." *Journal of Clinical Psychiatry*, 1984, *45*, 262–266.

Morgan, H. G., and Russell, G. F. "Value of Family Background and Clinical Features as Predictors of Long-Term Outcome in Anorexia Nervosa." *Psychological Medicine*, 1978, *5*, 355–371.

Rivinus, T. M., Biederman, J., Herzog, D. B., Kemper, K., Harper, G. P., Harmatz, J. S., and Houseworth, S. "Anorexia Nervosa and Affective Disorders: A Controlled Family History Study." *American Journal of Psychiatry*, 1984, *141*, 1414–1418.

Robins, E., and Guze, S. B. "Establishment of Diagnostic Validity in Psychiatric Illness." *American Journal of Psychiatry*, 1970, *126*, 983–987.

Steinhausen, H. C., and Glanville, K. "A Long-Term Follow-up of Adolescent Anorexia Nervosa: A Review of Research Findings." *Acta Psychiatrica Scandinavica*, 1983, *68*, 1–10.

Theander, S. "Anorexia Nervosa." *Acta Psychiatrica Scandinavica* (Supplement), 1970, *1*, 194–214.

Tolstrup, K., Brinch, M., Isager, T., Nielsen, S., Nystrup, J., Severin, B., and Olesen, N. S. "Long-Term Outcome of 151 Cases of Anorexia Nervosa." *Acta Psychiatrica Scandinavica*, 1985, *71*, 380–387.

Viesselman, J. O., and Roig, M. "Depression and Suicidality in Eating Disorders." *Journal of Clinical Psychiatry*, 1985, *46*, 118–124.

Winokur, A., March, A., and Mendels, J. "Primary Affective Disorder in Relatives of Patients with Anorexia Nervosa." *American Journal of Psychiatry*, 1980, *137* (6), 695–698.

Rodrigo A. Muñoz is clinical associate professor of psychiatry at the University of California, San Diego, and president, Western Mood & Sleep Disorders Institute, San Diego, California.

Henry Amado is assistant professor of psychiatry at Washington University in St. Louis, Missouri.

This chapter briefly reviews the role of the nutritionist in dealing with patients suffering from eating disorders, as conceived by Spitzer (1980).

Role of the Nutritionist in Eating Disorders

Johanna T. Dwyer

What Nutritionists Can Contribute to Effective Treatment

Nutritional-status assessment is important in establishing diagnosis, in evaluating treatment options as to degree of nutritional risk, and in overcoming potential barriers to nutritional treatment.

The nutritionists performs four essential assessment tasks: first, to document exactly which abnormal eating behaviors are present in each case; second, to review food intake data to obtain an estimate of intakes of energy, protein, vitamins, and minerals (intakes of nutrients from supplements should also be included); third, to take anthropometric measurements; and fourth, to draft a preliminary assessment of nutritional status for review by the physician.

Table 1 presents measurements that are useful in assessing nutritional status, as well as the rationale for each measurement. They are

This chapter was prepared with partial support from a grant by the Culpeper Foundation. The editorial assistance of Myra Monahan is also acknowledged with appreciation. The suggestions of Carol Stollar, M.Ed., R.D., Denise Arthurs, M.S., R.D., Mallai Holland, M.P.H., R.D., Beth Cornell, R.D., Sarah Carroll, R.N., M.S., and Linda Wetstein, R.D., were also helpful.

F.E.F. Larocca (ed.). *Eating Disorders.*
New Directions for Mental Health Services, no. 31. San Francisco: Jossey-Bass, Fall 1986.

Table 1. Nutritional Assessment of Patients
Suffering from Eating Disorders

Measurement	Rationale
Mandatory	
Diet Records	Provides some indicator of usual intakes
Height (measured) Elbow breadth Current weight in pounds as percent of desirable weight and as percent of usual (or predicted) weight	Useful for establishing desirable weight for target ranges
Minimal weight reached in adulthood as percent of usual or predicted weight	Needed to fulfill diagnostic criteria (25) for Anorexia Nervosa
Triceps skinfold Arm-muscle circumference	Helpful in assessing current body composition
Optional Arm-muscle circumference Creatinine-height index Serum albumin Estimated serum transferrin (TIBC mgm/100ml/1.45)	Provides indication of degree to which body protein stores (visceral and somatic) have been depleted and their possible functional defects
Immunocompetence measures Total lymphocytes Delayed hypersensitivity skin-testing common-recall antigens, such as Candida albicans, tubercular PPD, Trichophyton, streptokinase, streptodorinase	Indicates depletion of body protein stores.

described briefly here and in greater detail by Kovach (1982), Grant and others (1981), and McBurney and Wilmore (1981).

Food intakes, as obtained by diet history, show several patterns. Self-generated reports about food intake among anorectic patients are unreliable, but they usually suffice to identify which of the two major patterns are present: chronic starvation or starvation alternating with bingeing, purging, and vomiting (Dwyer, 1985; Herzog and Copeland, 1985; Huse and Lucas, 1984).

Patients who are not anorectic may exhibit patterns of extreme dieting alternating with bulimic episodes, along with an otherwise normal food intake pattern. Bingeing may occur by itself or with purging, diuretic or laxative abuse, or vomiting. Figure 1 shows the various abnormal eating behaviors that may be present in individual cases and the large number of different syndromes that may be involved.

Figure 1. Behaviors Involved in the Eating Disorders

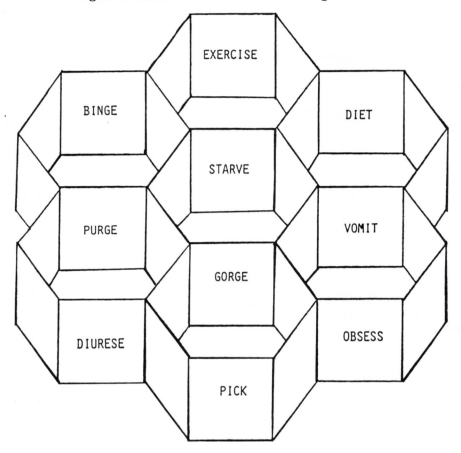

Anthropometric measurements are valuable both in making the nutritional diagnosis and in monitoring progress. Because patients suffering from eating disorders are so obsessive about their weight and fatness levels, it is important to take measurements carefully. Height should be measured and recorded and preferably taken in stocking feet, using a stadiometer (a movable board attached to a wall that permits more accurate measurement of height). Weight should be reported, using well-calibrated scales, only when the patient is weighed in underwear or a hospital wrap.

A measurement of frame is also helpful, since patients with eating disorders have distorted body images and they usually choose small frames, since this results in the lowest recommendation for desirable weight. Objective frame measurements, such as elbow breadth, can provide benchmarks that may be helpful later for setting appropriate targets for weight. Triceps skinfold measurements provide graphic evidence about the state of body fat stores. Other skinfolds may also be helpful in providing objective evidence that, in spite of what the patient may feel, she or he is not fat. Arm-muscle circumference measurements are a rough indicator of the lean body mass's contributions to build. Standards are available against which all these measurements can be compared (Frisancho, 1984; Metropolitan Height and Weight Tables, 1983).

The optimal measurements indicate the degree of wasting in somatic and visceral protein stores and of their effects on immune function. This is useful in the nutritional assessment of patients who are extremely underweight or malnourished and for whom special enteral or parenteral measures are being considered. Optional measures are usually necessary in underweight but healthy patients and are helpful in deciding about special nutritional support (Kovach, 1982; McBurney and Wilmore, 1981).

Helping the Patient Understand the Physiological Effects of the Eating Disorder

Although the physician may have outlined the physiological and psychological effects of the patient's eating practices, they merit repetition by the nutritionist. Most patients' views about food and nutrition are fraught with misconceptions.

Among patients suffering from anorexia and bulimia, the physical, endocrine, and psychological effects of starvation deserve particular emphasis (Dwyer, 1985; Harris, 1983; Herzog and Copeland, 1985). The loss of lean body mass eventually affects the function of skeletal, respiratory, and cardiac muscles, but patients may fail to connect it to their nutritional status. Resting metabolism also decreases, since the individual is in a hypocaloric state. Late in starvation, serum protein synthesis may decrease to such a point that normal fluid balance can no longer be maintained, so that edema results. Other changes in serum proteins jeopardize immune function, giving rise to secondary complications, such as infections. Patients often fail to understand that these physical problems result from their self-induced starvation (Cahill, 1970; Herzog and Copeland, 1985).

Helping the Patient Distinguish Between Healthy Dieting and the Eating Disorder

At the outset of treatment, the nutritionist needs to correct the common misconception among these patients that their eating disorder is simply a "reducing diet" gone awry. In fact, the diets of anorectics differ markedly from the diets prescribed by health professionals. Anorectic diets are more extreme with respect to their caloric reductions; more monotonous;

more ritualistic; more likely to be accompanied by body-image distortions and emotional and behavioral disorders; less nutritious; more time-consuming; and more likely to cause physical and psychological discomfort (Dwyer, 1985; Huse and Lucas, 1983, 1984). Also, weight loss is quantitatively and qualitatively different from that occurring on ordinary reducing diets. Quantitatively, in anorexia a much greater percentage of desirable body weight is lost and is lost faster. Qualitatively, the composition of weight lost differs (including more lean body mass), and the pattern is also abnormal in bulimia, fluctuating from losses to gains over a short time.

The most striking and obvious effect of Anorexia Nervosa is extreme weight loss, placing the patient at high risk. The total number of pounds of weight lost is a poor indication of risk, because obese patients can lose more weight without becoming emaciated than lean individuals can. Better indicators are the percentage of desirable body weight lost and the rate of loss, as well as number of pounds lost. The rate of weight loss gives further insight into the type of tissue that is being lost. Weight loss is rapid when the tissue being lost is lean tissue, which is low in energy but high in water and protein. A thousand-calorie deficit, when the patient is already emaciated and when lean tissue is being metabolized, leads to a weight loss of a pound or more, but if the patient is still fairly plump and mostly fat tissue is being lost, only a third of a pound or less will be lost. Rapid weight loss and low weight for height are signs of the loss of lean tissue, emaciation, and possible electrolyte imbalances, and so they are signs of impending danger in anorectics. Patients who are becoming emaciated need to be alerted to these facts.

Another misconception anorectics have about their diet is that the rituals they have adopted represent the only way they can avoid fatness. In fact, there are more effective ways to control weight. With professional dietetic help, weight control can be achieved at substantially less emotional and physical cost, leaving more time for the enjoyable aspects of life. For bulimics, too, a more effective individualized way can be found with professional help.

There is good evidence that laxative abuse is a relatively ineffective means of controlling body weight (Lacey and Gibson, 1985). Those who abuse laxatives for weight control need to be made aware of this. In one recent study, which contrasted purging and vomiting bulimics, purging bulimics' eating patterns generally involved excessive caloric intakes, but only a few hundred calories above the normal range. Purging was ineffective in controlling body weight because, in spite of daily laxative abuse, they weighed more than their desirable weight levels and more than bulimics who were vomiters. Laxatives apparently have little impact on intestinal absorption at the dosage used by the purgers. Other studies have shown that even with extreme purgation, only a relatively small percent (12 percent) of food energy ingested will be malabsorbed (Bo-Linn and others, 1983). The purgers apparently continue with their behaviors because laxative use gets rid of the food and, at least temporarily, lowers body weight—not because they experience permanent weight reductions. Purging shortens the time that the abdomen is distended after a bingeing episode, and it at least temporarily decreases weight because of excessive fecal water and electrolyte losses (Herzog and Copeland, 1985; Lacey, 1983; Lacey and Gibson, 1985). In addition to diarrhea and temporary dehydration, many purgers also suffer other undesirable side effects, including abdominal distention, pain, episodes of watery diarrhea at unpredictable times, and fluctuating edema.

In contrast to laxative abuse, vomiting is a temporarily more effective means of countering the consequences of binge-eating, but it does not provide a permanent solution. In Lacey and Gibson's (1985) study, vomiters ate significantly more than purgers, but they weighed less. The problem is that bulimics who indulge in vomiting often find that their appetites become even more voracious, and they soon develop the habit of consuming larger and larger amounts of food, sometimes up to three or more times normal intakes. This upward spiral of energy intake, and the physical and psychological side effects of ever more frequent vomiting, eventually result in medical and emotional difficulties, even if weight is temporarily controlled. Thus, vomiting has little to offer as a weight-control strategy.

What Nutritionists Should Avoid

Counseling Patients Who Lack Psychiatric or Medical Backup. It is always a mistake for the nutritionist to fancy herself a psychiatrist. Common pitfalls include initiating a confrontation with a patient without first discussing it with the therapist; getting entangled in alliances or disputes between the patient and other therapists; and forcing interactions between the patient and the members of the patient's family, without supervision. Nutritionists should not treat these patients unless they receive appropriate professional backup and consultations (Dwyer, 1985; Huse and Lucas, 1983, 1984).

Conflicts with the Patient. Some nutritionists simply lack the patience and forbearance necessary for dealing with patients suffering from eating disorders. Others have difficulties themselves with eating, which make it personally threatening for them to deal with patients whose eating is out of control. Some do better helping patients to begin to eat (as is necessary in anorexia), while others are more comfortable helping patients to stop eating (as in bulimia). Those to whom these characteristics apply should, for the patient's good as well as for their own, transfer care to another provider.

One-Time Visits. Parents and some physicians believe that the root cause of eating disorders is lack of nutrition education, but eating disorders do not result from a deficiency of nutritional knowledge that can be corrected by a visit to the dietitian. The barriers giving rise to nutritional problems are primarily emotional and are broken down only when the patient can summon the courage to change her diet and eating habits and eschew abnormal behaviors. Usually many visits to the dietitian are needed to do this, since changes must be gradual.

Expectations of Uninterrupted Progress. Eating disorders involve plateaus and occasional backsliding. When progress is interrupted, it should be viewed by the treatment team as a temporary, usual occurrence that may be overcome.

Threatening Anorectics Who Refuse to Eat. The dietitian should never threaten the anorectic patient with tube or parenteral feedings. Patients may become so fearful that they drop out of treatment entirely. In any event, such threats fail to motivate most patients. If it becomes necessary to consider special enteral or parenteral nutrition therapies or hospitalization, a medical consultation is in order (Chiulli and others, 1982; Dempsey and others, 1984; Grant and others, 1981; Kovach, 1982; McBurney and Wilmore, 1981; Meguid and others, 1981).

Overfeeding at First. Excessive zeal to restore nutritional health can sometimes lead nutritionists to overfeed anorectics early in their treatment. This often frightens patients and causes resistance. It is better to settle for small nutritional increments on a daily basis and to gain the patients' trust (Huse and Lucas, 1983, 1984).

Catering Excessively to the Anorectic's Whims. It is important to individualize the anorectic's dietary prescriptions. There is a limit, however, to how much catering can be done. The general principle is that the patient should eat what is served in the hospital, and that any objections will be discussed and resolved at the next nutritional interview, not by rejecting food. The nursing and food service staffs should be instructed that if the patient does refuse to eat an item, its calorie equivalent should be added to the next meal.

Conclusion

The nutritionist's expertise in diet therapy, food habits, and food composition, as well as her experience in assisting patients in achieving planned dietary change, can be helpful in the treatment of the eating disorders. Without concomitant psychotherapy, however, little permanent change is likely to be accomplished.

References

Bo-Linn, G. W., Santa Ana, C. A., Morawski, S. G., and Fordtran, J. S. "Purging and Calorie Absorption in Bulimic Patients and Normal Women." *Annals of Internal Medicine,* 1983, *99,* 14–26.

Cahill, G. F. "Starvation in Men." *New England Journal of Medicine*, 1970, *282*, 668–675.

Chiulli, R., Grover, M., and Steiger, E. "Total Parenteral Nutrition in Anorexia Nervosa." In M. Gross (ed.), *Anorexia Nervosa: A Comprehensive Approach.* Lexington: The Collamore Press, 1982.

Dempsey, D. T., Crosby, L. O., Lusk, E., Oberlander, J. L., Pertshuk, M. J., and Mullen, J. L. "Total Body Water and Total Body Potassium in Anorexia Nervosa." *American Journal of Clinical Nutrition*, 1984, *40*, 260–269.

Dwyer, J. "Nutritional Aspects of Anorexia Nervosa and Bulimia." In S. Emmett (ed.), *Theory and Treatment of Anorexia Nervosa.* New York: Brunner Mazel, 1985.

Frisancho, A. R. "New Standards of Weight and Body Composition by Frame Size and Height for Assessment of Nutritional Status of Adults and the Elderly." *American Journal of Clinical Nutrition*, 1984, *40*, 808–819.

Grant, J. P., Custer, P. B., and Thurlow, J. "Current Techniques of Nutritional Assessment." *Surgical Clinics of North America*, 1981, *61*, 437–463.

Harris, R. T. "Bulimarexia and Related Serious Eating Disorders with Medical Complications." *Annals of Internal Medicine*, 1983, *99*, 800–807.

Herzog, D. B., and Copeland, P. M. "Eating Disorders." *New England Journal of Medicine*, 1985, *313*, 295–303.

Huse, D. M., and Lucas, A. R. "Dietary Treatment of Anorexia Nervosa." *Journal of the American Dietetic Association*, 1983, *83*, 687–690.

Huse, D. M., and Lucas, A. R. "Dietary Patterns in Anorexia Nervosa." *American Journal of Clinical Nutrition*, 1984, *40*, 251–254.

Kovach, K. M. "The Assessment of Nutritional Status in Anorexia Nervosa." In M. Gross (ed.), *Anorexia Nervosa: A Comprehensive Approach.* Lexington: The Collamore Press, 1982.

Lacey, J. H. "Bulimia Nervosa, Binge Eating, and Psychogenic Vomiting: A Controlled Treatment Study and Long-Term Outcome." *British Medical Journal*, 1983, *286*, 1609–1613.

Lacey, J. H., and Gibson, E. "Does Laxative Abuse Control Body Weight? A Comparative Study of Purging and Vomiting Bulimics." *Human Nutrition: Applied Nutrition*, 1985, *39A*, 36–42.

McBurney, M., and Wilmore, D. W. "Rational Decision-Making in Nutritional Care." *Surgical Clinics of North America*, 1981, *61*, 571–582.

Meguid, M. M., Collier, M. D., and Howard, L. J. "Uncomplicated and Stressed Starvation." *Surgical Clinics of North America*, 1981, *61*, 529–543.

Metropolitan Height and Weight Tables. *Statistical Bulletin*, 1983, *64*, 1–9.

Spitzer, R. L. (ed.). *Task Force on Nomenclature and Statistics: Diagnostic and Statistical Manual of Mental Disorders* (3rd ed.). Washington, D.C.: American Psychiatric Association, 1980.

Johanna T. Dwyer is professor of medicine (nutrition) at Tufts Medical School and director of the Frances Stern Nutrition Center, New England Medical Center Hospitals, Boston, Massachusetts.

*This chapter describes eating disorders outside the most typical
clinical presentations in female adolescents and young adult
women. Of some importance is the association of eating
disorders with some relatively rare conditions, and of specific
relevance is Anorexia Nervosa in children and older females.*

Atypical Eating Disorders

Barton J. Blinder, Stanley L. Goodman

Anorexia and bulimia, the two major eating disorders, are most prevalent
in adolescent and young adult females. Anorexia Nervosa is characterized
by a relentless pursuit of thinness, an almost delusional disturbance of
body image, and an inability to correctly identify hunger from other bodily
attention states. In addition, there is an inability to maintain a body
weight, a previous 25 percent weight loss, a lack of identity awareness,
and a paralyzing sense of ineffectiveness. This sense of ineffectiveness,
which pervades thought and action, is connected with a feeling that the
self acts only in response to the demands of others. The inability to experience control over one's own body is based on deficits of autonomy and
initiative, originating from a distortion and mislabeling of feelings, sensations, and moods in early childhood. Treatment of anorectics focuses on
improving the awareness that their impulsive feelings and needs originate
within themselves as part of a step in the development of a sense of
competence and self-esteem (Bruch, 1981).

The characteristic behavioral pattern of bulimia includes the sur-
repetitious ingestion of large quantities of food, usually carbohydrates,
diuretics, or syrup of ipecac, as a desperate attempt to maintain body
weight (Ferguson, 1985). While bulimia is sometimes a symptom of obesity
or Anorexia Nervosa, it is frequently encountered in patients with normal
weight. Detection may be problematic, since secrecy and shame accompany
this syndrome. Diagnostic clues for identifying bulimic patients include

F.E.F. Larocca (ed.). *Eating Disorders.*
New Directions for Mental Health Services, no. 31. San Francisco: Jossey-Bass, Fall 1986.

preoccupation with weight, gastrointestinal complaints, dental and oro-pharyngeal changes, salivary gland enlargement, edema and bloating, amenorrhea, dermatological complaints, substance abuse, laboratory changes, and serious consequences (Winstead and Willard, 1983).

This chapter discusses the presentation of these disorders in children and in females beyond age twenty-five.

Anorexia Nervosa in Children

Anorexia Nervosa has been reported beginning at age four (Gislason, 1986). Childhood anorexia should fulfill criteria for adolescent or adult-onset anorexia, except that in children, because of a diminished amount of body fat, a twenty-five percent weight loss is not necessary. In female childhood cases, primary amenorrhea occurs. The incidence of prepubertal Anorexia Nervosa is estimated at 3 percent of the total cases reported. Females comprise 73 percent of all reported childhood cases.

Development of childhood anorexia has not been systematically researched. Delaney and Silber (1984) evaluated approximately thirty cases and noted lack of typical negativism at age two, clinging behavior upon commencement of school, and difficulty maintaining peer relations, resulting in social isolation.

In infants ages nine months to twenty-six months, Chatoor and Egan (1983) described the development disturbance that they consider to be a separation disorder and a form of infantile anorexia. These infants were noted to have a diminished growth rate, and they refused food. Feeding became the battleground for maternal-infant autonomy. The infants resisted feeding as a manifestation of independence from an overwhelmingly strong maternal figure. The child's fight for independence through anorectic behavior is sharply contrasted to the listless marasmic pattern that characterized the anorexia in anaclitic depression (Spitz and Wolf, 1946).

Latency-age children, at the Piagetian stage of concrete thinking, conceptualize food and water together as one entity. A resulting global ingestive restriction may lead to rapid weight loss and serious dehydration. In addition, prepubertal children, especially girls, have less body fat than their adolescent counterparts and become more quickly emaciated. In Irwin's (1984) series, over two-thirds of the children with anorexia were hospitalized within six months of the onset of anorexia, and Gislason (1986) noted that 4 percent died.

Sargent and Liebman (1984) described three subgroups of prepubertal anorectics. The first group, similar to the one described by Pugliese and others (1983), severely restricted food intake, with resulting short stature. They had fears of becoming obese, and by their deficient weight gain they maintained both a physical and psychological immaturity. The second group consisted primarily of prepubertal females, ages ten to twelve, who were psychologically pseudoprecocious, engaging in overt behavior more characteristic of that of a prepubescent fourteen-year-old. However, underneath this facade, they were described as "lost little girls." Their parents did not want them to be younger children and strongly encouraged their pseudoadolescent behavior. This female subgroup is closest to the pubertal-onset Anorexia Nervosa profile. The third subgroup consisted of an equal number of male and female anorectics who were more psychologically impaired, having major ego deficits, with the occasional presence of psychotic episodes (Falstein and others, 1956).

The clinical manifestation of childhood Anorexia Nervosa should fulfill most established diagnostic criteria. However, since prepubertal children, especially girls, have less body fat than their adolescent counterparts, a 15 percent reduction in body weight should be sufficient for diagnosis. These children, while recognizing their thinness, deny feeling fat. It is unclear whether there is a body-image distortion similar to that of older anorectics. Furthermore, no studies on children have been undertaken. Children may be more concerned with separation-individuation issues than with fears of sexuality (Irwin, 1984). They frequently demonstrate alexithymia, the inability to translate feelings into words.

Many children with Anorexia Nervosa manifested signs of depression. These feelings may be secondary to helplessness and ineffectiveness in this chronic disorder. Studies reported prior to DSM-III did not utilize structured interviews, such as Kiddie SADS. In anorectic children, no formalized studies ascertaining biochemical, diagnostic, or family criteria for major depressive disorders have been reported. While Anorexia Nervosa has been considered a variant of affective disorder (Cantwell and others, 1977), the relationship between childhood Anorexia Nervosa and affective disorder is unclear.

Anorexia Nervosa has been associated with Tourette's syndrome, the stereotyped-movement disorder (Blinder and others, 1984; Larocca, 1984); with Turner's syndrome, a chromosome disorder with XO genotype and gonadal dysgenesis (Larocca, 1985); and with mental retardation (Hurley and Sovner, 1979).

The etiology of childhood anorexia is uncertain. Irwin (1984) feels the dynamics in childhood Anorexia Nervosa are similar to the dynamics of adolescent-onset anorexia and include identity disturbance, failure of separation-individuation with fears of growing up, maladaptive attempts to be in control, and failure to resolve marital or family conflicts. Another variation includes the case of a child who is sensitive to the family's food preoccupation, identifying with a family member who has an eating disturbance.

Precipitating events associated with the onset of childhood Anorexia Nervosa include the birth of a sibling; bereavement over the death of a parent or other relative; a disappointment in object relations; family discord; viral illness; peer criticism about being fat; the fear of becoming obese; the onset of breast development; sexual abuse; sustained fear of choking while eating; anticipated fear of parental loss, related to an ill or depressed parent; and the onset of a psychophysiological disorder, such as ulcerative colitis (Gislason, 1986).

In the treatment of the childhood anorectic, the therapist should work closely with a pediatrician to rule out medical and psychological conditions producing anorexia. A physical examination and laboratory studies are mandatory to monitor starvation effects, which include hypotension, syncope, hypothermia, dry skin, lanugo hair, diminished triceps skin-fold thickness, hypoglycemia, hair loss, sensitivity to noise, leukopenia, fatigue, arrhythmia, electrolyte and hypothalamic dysfunction, gastric ulcer, and hyperactivity. Starvation can cause psychological and cognitive disturbances, including food preoccupation, poor concentration, social isolation, depression, and labile moods (Maloney and Klykylo, 1983).

Anorexia Nervosa has been reported in prepubertal children, many of whom appear to be more disturbed than are adolescents with the same disorder. The precise etiology is uncertain, but life events centering on losses and separation may be onset factors in Anorexia Nervosa. Due to less body fat and restriction of both food and water, this disorder may be more ominous in children, necessitating a rapid and vigorous therapy and frequently requiring inpatient treatment. Prognosis is guarded and uncertain. Further coexistent medical illnesses, colitis, or ileitis with Anorexia Nervosa require a careful physical examination.

Atypical Bulimic Disorders in Children

In the current literature, there have been no reports of childhood bulimia in association with purging. Prepubertal children may not be sufficiently sophisticated to purge; or, possibly, latency-age girls are less vulnerable to the social pressure to be thin. Case histories of two males having many characteristics of bulimia, including impulsivity and binge episodes, are presented here.

Two case reports (Atkinson, personal communication, 1985) of male bulimia indicated global impulsiveness, learning disability, and, in one case, possible attention-deficit disorder. Patient J, age fourteen, who was of Russian-Jewish extraction, had engaged in daily binges since the age of ten. He ate huge quantities of all types of food, especially carbohydrates. His bingeing began soon after he emigrated with his parents from Russia to Canada. His parents were rarely home, a fact indicating that he sustained a partial object-loss. Exhibiting aggressive, threatening behavior, he was referred by the school for help. In addition, he was found to have a learning disability. Although he appeared depressed, he denied affective symptoms, either during the day or after his binges, and did not offer reasons for terminating them. He worried about his weight and recognized that his bingeing was abnormal, but he was unable to diet. He continued to binge, remained obese, and appeared markedly depressed. He denied heterosexual interest.

In the second case, the death of Kyle's father was associated with the onset of his bingeing at age eleven. These episodes occurred several times a week, while he was either alone (usually) or with his mother (rarely). He consumed huge amounts of carbohydrates and terminated with the onset of abdominal pain. He was aware that these episodes were abnormal and wanted to lose weight. He considered himself obese, but he felt helpless and despondent at not having the inner control to diet. However, weight fluctuations were present. His father had an eating disturbance manifested by vomiting and later by inanition prior to his death from cancer. Kyle's mother also had a cerebral vascular accident and had difficulty functioning. He reported that there was marked parental discord before his father's death.

Kyle had features of attention-deficit disorder and, because of his global impulsiveness, he was later placed in a locked facility. Bingeing episodes have continued for three years to the present time, and he denies heterosexual interest.

These cases of latency bingeing in males have characteristics of bulimia, including a wish to be thin, recognition of the abnormality of the bingeing, frequent bingeing episodes, and, in one patient, termination by abdominal pain. The bingeing was not due to Anorexia Nervosa or to any other known physical disorders. While the patients usually binged alone, bingeing would sometimes occur in the mother's presence. While they wanted to diet, they did not have sufficient motivation. The impulsiveness of these two patients is striking, and this characteristic has also been reported in female bulimia (Mitchell and Goff, 1984).

The relationship between affective disturbance and eating disorders is unclear in these cases. However, a complete object-loss of father (Kyle) and partial object-loss of both parents because of excess work hours (J) appear as associated findings. Family crisis and instability are also present.

Anorexia Nervosa in Females over Age Twenty-Five

Anorexia Nervosa may occur after age twenty-five in females (Dally, 1984; Price and others, 1985; Vandereycken and others, 1986). The oldest reported case was of a sixty-eight-year-old woman with no history of eating disturbance. The incidence of Anorexia Nervosa in old age is unknown. Fewer than a hundred patients, both male and female, have been reported in the world's literature (Dally, 1984; Ryle, 1936; Kellett and others, 1976; Launer, 1978). Adult-onset cases usually come from upper-middle-class families.

Precipitating factors of Anorexia Nervosa in susceptible patients include multiple surgical procedures or illness (Ryle, 1936), stress secondary to childbirth or marriage (Kellett and others, 1976), and death of a spouse (Price and others, 1985).

In married anorectics whose dependency needs have been shifted to their children, the children's absence resulting from moving or marriage has been associated with an acute onset of anorexia.

Sexual abuse may be involved in the development of Anorexia Nervosa in susceptible women. Leichner and others (in press) recently reported six cases of hospitalized anorectic adults who were sexually abused as children or adolescents. Adult patients may have felt ashamed or embarrassed and may have defended the abuse because of intense superego pressures; only later in therapy would they admit to the sexual harassment. At the onset of puberty, sexual impulses were defended against by an anorectic regression to latency.

A variety of onset patterns has been described. The most common pattern is one in which the patient has a chronic eating disturbance or peculiar eating habits, and a stress produces a full-blown case of Anorexia Nervosa. In other patients, an anorectic episode may have occurred during adolescence, followed by a long remission; stressful events again precipitate anorexia. The most uncommon pattern is that of an adult patient who develops anorexia de novo (Vandereycken and others, 1986). The therapist needs to obtain a very detailed history of the patient's early eating patterns and determine whether a prior episode occurred.

Some patients who exhibit pure restrictive anorexia develop bulimia during or after treatment. Failure of appetite or restraints may first occur in bulimic episodes. Vandereycken and others (1986) suggest that some anorectics who fail treatment develop vomiting, purging, or frank bulimia. Kellett and others (1976) described a fifty-two-year-old woman who purged and vomited in addition to exhibiting anorexia.

Vandereycken and others (1986) conceptualize anorexia as an incurable illness in some patients, with spontaneously occurring remission and exacerbation. This chronic course, seen in older patients, is a form of process Anorexia Nervosa, as differentiated from a more reactive, self-limited disorder seen in younger, mainly adolescent patients. Furthermore, Vandereycken and others compare anorexia, with or without bulimia, to an addiction, with the development of malignant autonomy, apparent physical dependency, social descent, and physical ruin.

Although some patients with late-onset chronic Anorexia Nervosa may recover after intensive treatment, patients failing to maintain weight at four- to eight-year follow-ups may have to be supported in the decision to remain anorectic. In these cases, the goal of treatment is to minimize the physical and emotional handicaps of the disease.

Vandereycken and others (1986) raise the ethical questions concerning treatment of chronic anorectics and bulimics. Although the patients may feel life is barren with anorexia, life may become even more barren and painful without it. Furthermore, chronic bulimics can organize their lives around the bulimia. Bulimic episodes can become institutionalized, with some patients indulging in "controlled binges in gourmet restaurants."

Women beyond age twenty-five who develop anorexia and whose physical examinations are normal should be screened for Anorexia Nervosa.

Bulimia in Females Beyond Age Twenty-Five

Bulimia may be under-reported in women over age twenty-five. Population surveys have uncovered few older bulimic patients. Jonas and others (1984) reported a fifty-six-year-old woman with rapid-cycling bipolar disorder and unexplained vomiting. She had no prior history of an eating disorder, and during hospitalization the staff discovered surreptitious vomiting. Bulimia disappeared with individual medication trials, first with imipramine, then with phenelzine.

Older patients with affective disorder and unexplained vomiting not secondary to psychotropic drug toxicity should be screened for bulimia. Because of electrolyte disturbance, lithium may be hazardous or lethal in patients with self-induced, surreptitious vomiting. Patients taking lithium for bipolar disorder, emotionally unstable character disorder, or recurrent unipolar depression should be screened for bulimia. Bipolar patients with bulimia may respond to carbamazepine (Kaplan and others, 1983). The prevalence of bulimia in older patients with both affective disorder and unexplained vomiting should be explored to minimize the medical complications of bulimia, especially in patients treated with lithium.

The presentation of the eating disorders Anorexia Nervosa and bulimia in atypical forms, as in association with rare conditions or with earlier or later onset than expected by formally established diagnostic criteria, further underscores the complexity of this widespread issue.

References

Blinder, B. J., Caswell-Papillon, L., and Sukin, P. J. "Anorexia Nervosa and Tourette's Syndrome." Paper presented at International Conference on Eating Disorders, New York City, 1984.

Bruch, H. "Developmental Considerations of Anorexia Nervosa and Obesity." *Canadian Journal of Psychiatry*, 1981, *4*, 212–217.

Cantwell, D. P., Sturzenberger, S., Burroughs, J., Salkin, B., and Green, J. K. "Anorexia Nervosa: An Affective Disorder?" *Archives of General Psychiatry*, 1977, *34*, 1087–1093.

Chatoor, I., and Egan, J. "A Nonorganic Failure to Thrive and Dwarfism Due to Food Refusal: A Separation Disorder." *Journal of Academic Child Psychiatry*, 1983, *22*, 294–301.

Dally, R. "Anorexia Tardive-Late Onset Marital Anorexia Nervosa." *Journal of Psychosomatic Research*, 1984, *28*, 423–428.

Delaney, D., and Silber, T. J. "Treatment of Anorexia Nervosa in a Pediatric Program." *Pediatric Annals*, 1984.

Falstein, E. I., Feinstein, S. C., and Judas, I. "Anorexia Nervosa in the Male Child." *American Journal of Orthopsychiatry*, 1956, *26*, 751–770.

Ferguson, J. M. "Bulimia: A Potentially Fatal Syndrome." *Journal of Academic Psychosomatic Medicine*, 1985, *26*, 252–253.

Gislason, L. I. "Eating Disorders in Childhood Ages 4 Through 11 Years." In B. J. Blinder, B. F. Chaitin, and others (eds.), *Modern Concepts of the Eating Disorder: Diagnosis, Treatment, Research*. Jamaica, N.Y.: Spectrum Publications, 1986.

Hurley, A. D., and Sovner, R. "Anorexia Nervosa and Mental Retardation: A Case Report." *Journal of Clinical Psychiatry*, 1979, *40*, 480–481.

Irwin, M. "Early Onset Anorexia Nervosa." *Southern Medical Journal*, 1984, *77*, 611–614.

Jonas, J. M., Pope, H. G., Hudson, J. I., and Satlin, A. "Undiagnosed Vomiting in an Older Woman: Unsuspected Bulimia." *American Journal of Psychiatry*, 1984, *141*, 902.

Kaplan, A. S., Garfinkel, P. E., Darby, P. L., and Garner, D. M. "Carbamazepine in the Treatment of Bulimia." *American Journal of Psychiatry*, 1983, *140* (9), 1225–1226.

Kellett, J., Trimble, M., and Thorley, A. "Anorexia Nervosa After the Menopause." *British Journal of Psychiatry*, 1976, *128*, 555–558.

Larocca, F.E.F. "Gilles de la Tourette's (The Movement Disorder): The Association with a Case of Anorexia Nervosa in a Boy." *International Journal of Eating Disorders*, 1984, *3*, 89–93.

Larocca, F.E.F. "Concurrence of Turner's Syndrome, Anorexia Nervosa, and Mood Disorders: A Case Report." *Journal of Clinical Psychiatry*, 1985, *46*, 296–297.

Launer, M. A. "Anorexia Nervosa in Late Life." *British Journal of Medical Psychology*, 1978, *51*, 375–377.

Leichner, P., Arnett, J., Srikaneswaran, S., and others. "Screening for Anorexia Nervosa and Bulimia in a Canadian School Age Population." *Canadian Medical Journal*, in press.

Maloney, M. J., and Klykylo, W. M. "An Overview of Anorexia Nervosa, Bulimia, and Obesity in Children and Adolescents." *Journal of the American Academy of Child Psychiatry*, 1983, *22*, 99–107.

Mitchell, J. E., and Goff, G. "Bulimia in Male Patients." *Psychosomatics*, 1984, *25*, 909–913.

Price, W., Giannini, J. A., and Colella, J. "Anorexia Nervosa in the Elderly." *Journal of the American Geriatrics Society*, 1985, *33*, 213–215.

Pugliese, M. T., Lifshitz, F., Grad, G., Fort, P., and Marks-Katz, M. "Fear of Obesity: Cause of Short Stature and Delayed Puberty." *New England Journal of Medicine*, 1983, *309*, 513–518.

Ryle, J. A. "Anorexia Nervosa." *Lancet*, 1936, *1*, 893–899.

Sargent, J. and Liebman, R. "Outpatient Treatment of Anorexia Nervosa." *Psychiatric Clinics of North America*, 1984, 7 (2), 235–245.

Spitz, R. A., and Wolf, K. M. "Anaclitic Depression: An Inquiry into the Genesis of Psychiatric Conditions in Early Infancy." In *The Psychoanalytic Study of the Child*. Vol. 2. New York: International University Press, 1946.

Vandereycken, W. "Anorexia Nervosa in Adults." In B. J. Blinder, B. F. Chaitin, and others (eds.), *Modern Concepts of the Eating Disorder: Diagnosis, Treatment, Research*. Jamaica, N.Y.: Spectrum Publications, 1986.

Winstead, D. K., and Willard, S. G. "Bulimia: Diagnostic Clues." *Southern Medical Journal*, 1983, *76*, 313–315.

Barton J. Blinder is associate clinical professor of psychiatry and director, Eating Disorders Program and Research Studies, Department of Psychiatry and Human Behavior, University of California College of Medicine in Irvine, California.

Stanley L. Goodman is a research associate in Irvine, California.

Males with eating disorders share with female patients many aspects of diagnosis, psychopathology, and treatment, but they present significant differences in pre-illness weight, mode of onset, and psychotherapeutic needs.

Males with Eating Disorders

Arnold E. Andersen

Overview of Current State of Knowledge

The first widely accepted clinical description of Anorexia Nervosa clearly stated that the disorder occurs in males (Morton, 1694), a fact that was restated by Sir William Gull (1874), the nineteenth-century rediscoverer of the disorder. The presence of anorexia in males was ignored or lost sight of for the first half of this century by many clinicians for several reasons. Some theoreticians believed that the "fear of oral impregnation" was the essential psychodynamic motif for the disorder, thereby excluding males, who would not be expected to produce this theme in therapy. The disorder was relatively uncommon, with many practitioners not being confident of the diagnosis in females, much less in males. Some diagnostic criteria included amenorrhea, thereby again excluding males.

Bulimia, the companion disorder to Anorexia Nervosa, has been well described for only the past ten years. Reports of the incidence and descriptive psychopathology of males with bulimia are only now finding their way slowly into the literature. Bulimia is best seen as part of a spectrum of eating disorders. It may occur with any degree of weight loss or in an individual with normal or above-normal weight.

The following data summarize generally accepted information about eating disorders in males at present. First and most important, cases do exist. Andersen and Mickalide (1983) noted that 24 patients in 214

F.E.F. Larocca (ed.). *Eating Disorders.*
New Directions for Mental Health Services, no. 31. San Francisco: Jossey-Bass, Fall 1986.

consecutive referrals to an eating- and weight-disorders clinic were males. This incidence of about 10 percent reappears in a number of other reports. The diagnosis is made by the same criteria as in females, with only a slight modification. The essential features of diagnosis in Anorexia Nervosa are self-induced starvation, fear of fatness from loss of control over eating, and amenorrhea. This last criterion, amenorrhea, is more appropriately generalized to include abnormalities in reproductive hormone functioning. Bulimia is diagnosed in patients who do not meet the criteria for anorexia by weight but who do experience binge-eating in a compulsive manner, followed by attempts to avoid weight gain by methods such as vomiting, abuse of laxatives or diuretics, fasting, or exercise.

Weight loss as great as that occurring in anorexia is found in about 25 percent of the cases, and they are thought to be due to other psychiatric complications, especially psychogenic dysphagia, schizophrenia, psychophysiological reactions, and anxiety states. No large population studies have been conducted to give good epidemiological descriptions of males with eating disorders, but preliminary studies suggest that the usually accepted ten-to-one ratio of females to males is relatively accurate. There is an increasing incidence of anorexia and bulimia in the higher social classes, but no class is excluded from having these disorders.

A number of subgroups within the population appear to be especially vulnerable to these disorders. Jockeys, wrestlers, dancers, and entertainers often are required to lose weight to achieve vocational goals. We have found that medical students represent a vulnerable population, with the incidence in males being many times that found in the general population.

Affective disorders occur more frequently in the families of males suffering from eating disorder than they do in control groups. A common predisposing feature is an obsessional perfectionistic personality.

With respect to the age of onset, it may be helpful to divide males with anorexia into three groups. The youngest group, those under thirteen, appears to have fewer distinctive features individually and more global distress in the family. Males ten to twenty-five years old with anorexia or bulimia have many of the features of these disorders found in females but differ in their modes of presentation. They are generally less conscious of wanting to achieve a certain weight or a certain size in clothing but are more conscious of muscle definition and of the avoidance of any flab. The group with onset age above twenty-five may be confused with patients having other psychiatric or biological disorders associated with weight loss, such as depression or cancer, and the diagnosis is often missed.

In at least some significant areas, males differ from females having the same diagnoses. As a group, males are more likely to have been actually overweight rather than to feel overweight prior to the onset of dieting.

On the average, males were 21 percent above ideal weight prior to dieting, as compared to the females who began in the normal range. Because of this history of being overweight, they were often teased or criticized for lacking self-control. In general, the desire to increase self-esteem through change in body size and shape is the strongest motivation for dieting among males. A small percentage of patients loses weight for essentially medical rather than cosmetic reasons. Some take dieting to an extreme because they have been warned so severely by doctors about the dangers of being overweight, sometimes because of the diseases associated with excess weight among family members. Another small group may exercise to lose weight following an illness or accident that caused their initial weight loss. Some of our male patients, usually those in their mid-teenage years or older, desire to lose weight to become more attractive to heterosexual or homosexual partners. Some of the older males began losing weight after their supervisors at work asked them to improve their appearance in order to gain promotions. Some started losing weight in an effort to slow down the process of aging as the midlife years approached.

Males with bulimia share many of the motivating influences of those having anorexia. Bulimia commonly begins in response to hunger secondary to severe dieting. What initially starts out as a response to hunger then generalizes to become an all-purpose mechanism for dealing with a variety of uncomfortable mood states. Binges first serve to respond to hunger and then later respond to anger, depression, boredom, and other kinds of dysphoria.

In their classic book, Keys and others (1950) describe many of the nonspecific changes that occur in individuals who lose weight. In this particular population, they induced a moderate degree of starvation of more than 20 percent weight loss in male volunteers. These individuals exhibited social isolation, preoccupation with food, and many of the behaviors typical of anorectic patients—hoarding food and cutting it into very small pieces, for example. Their experiment showed that many of the symptoms of Anorexia Nervosa are not related to psychodynamic issues but to the effects of semistarvation.

Endocrinological aspects of these cases have revealed that LH and FSH are decreased in females. In females, this may result in cessation of the menstrual flow and in the male a gradual decline in reproductive functioning and to a decrease in flow of circulating testosterone in proportion to decreasing body weight.

LH and FSH are decreased in both males and females. In contrast to females, who have an on-off phenomenon with loss of menstrual periods, males show a gradual decline in their reproductive functioning. There is a decrease in circulating testosterone in proportion to the decrease in weight. As a result, there is a concomitant decrease in sexual interest, drive, and performance.

Principal Concepts and Issues from a Theoretical Perspective

There are at least four key questions concerning a theoretical understanding of eating disorders in males: Why do so few males develop Anorexia Nervosa? Does it occur in a different form in males, so that its true incidence is not realized? What is the sexual orientation and practice of males with eating disorders—are they all homosexual or bisexual? What makes these males vulnerable to these disorders?

An argument has been made that fewer males develop anorexia because they are biologically protected or lack the biological vulnerabilities of females. This remains an intriguing hypothesis, but one that lacks scientific confirmation. For example, there is no evidence that having steady gonadotropic levels protects a male. The fact that males have larger muscle mass is a reflection of their testosterone and does not in itself constitute a protection from anorexia.

A persuasive argument can be made that fewer males have anorexia or bulimia because there is much less sociocultural emphasis on thinness in males; there are no male role models comparable to Twiggy. Magazines that have primarily male readers do not emphasize dieting and weight control to the extent that these issues are found in women's magazines. There is much less peer pressure for thinness in males. In fact, the opposite may occur; many adolescent males may wish to increase their muscle bulk. Of course, some exceptions do occur, such as in males who work in fashion industries or who are dancers. Currently, the diminished pressure on males to become slim persists throughout life and never reaches the intensity experienced by females.

Yates and others (1983) have argued that compulsively running males may represent a form of anorexia. There is certainly an overlap between compulsive runners and anorectics, but, in general, compulsive runners are simply compulsive, rather than anorectic. The vast majority of male runners simply do not have self-induced starvation or fear of fatness, beyond desiring a thin normal weight range.

Our experience regarding the sexual practices of male anorectics and bulimics suggests that they are similar to female patients in a number of ways. Little data exist on the preteenage sexual behavior of these patients. Male teenagers with anorexia more often than not are sexually immature and intellectually oriented, having little sexual experience and feeling guilty about sexual thoughts and practices. By the mid-teenage years, some male anorectics experience crisis in sexual orientation, with questions about gender identity and sexual roles. The majority, however, are not homosexual but tend rather to be obsessional, perfectionistic, and insecure in their sexuality.

Older males with eating disorders tend to have a clearer sexual orientation, and the majority remain heterosexual. Many of them, however, are not truly relaxed and comfortable with their sexual lives. We have found that several of our patients, despite normal weight, had lowered testosterone or decreased sperm production.

What makes certain males vulnerable to developing Anorexia Nervosa or bulimia? The issue of symptom choice in psychodynamic psychiatry has never been adequately resolved. We are working with the hypothesis that males who develop anorexia have a higher incidence of obsessional disorders and obsessional personalities in their families than males who do not develop anorexia. Bulimic males often share these features but, in addition, they tend to be more dramatic and narcissistic and to have borderline features. Bulimic males as well as females show an increased incidence of problem behaviors, such as promiscuity, drug abuse, alcoholism, and self-harm. A general distinction may be made between basically normal individuals who have a "bulimic problem" and individuals who are globally disturbed.

Research-Based Analyses of Major Problems

There are relatively few papers on males with eating disorders, but more are appearing all the time. A few studies are worth mentioning. Burns and Crisp (1984) followed twenty-seven consecutive males treated for anorexia for up to twenty years after presentation. They found that 44 percent had good outcomes, having attained healthy weight and normal sexual functioning. In the study, 26 percent had intermediate outcome and 30 percent poor outcome, with low weight and poor or no sexual activity. The poorest outcome was associated with longer duration of illness, past treatment, and greater severity of weight loss. A disturbed relationship with parents in childhood and the absence of normal sexual behavior in adolescence were also predictive of poor outcome.

Herzog and others (1984) found more sexual isolation, sexual inactivity, and conflicted homosexuality in males with anorexia or bulimia. They reported 26 percent of their patients to have homosexual orientation. Gwirtsman and Gerner (1981) found that all their patients showed abnormalities of liver enzymes and amylase. Two out of three had nonsuppression of dexamethosone, and one had a blunted TH response to TRH. Each of these patients had at least one abnormality in neuroendocrine functioning. Each of the patients was described as being impulsive, with some antisocial behaviors, and two or three had abused drugs or alcohol.

Nylander (1971) documented that in Sweden teenage males in general were less preoccupied with dieting than females were. This is one of the few studies that gives specific numbers to a general impression that males are less sensitive to issues of weight. Others have noted a much smaller percentage of male college students having bulimic behavior than female college students.

Summary and Conclusions

Physicians learn in medical school that they cannot diagnose a disorder they do not think about. This is most commonly said in regard to appendicitis but also applies to eating disorders. All clinicians must remember that anorexia and bulimia can and do occur in males, and that it may appear in different forms than it does in females. Diagnosis is made by finding the association of fears of fatness, excessive dieting, and binge-purge practices.

Each male with an eating disorder should be treated individually. Myths and stereotypes must be set aside in these treatments. A number of specific male-oriented issues need to be addressed.

Sexuality. The most general problem regarding sexuality is that of alexithymia. Many of these patients have difficulty in identifying and describing feelings of any type, including sexual ones. Treatment for the sexual aspects of these disorders begins with much-needed information about sexual and social functioning. Patients are often too insecure to ask for needed information, and so the staff should approach them in an emphatic, direct manner. While information about sexual maturation and bodily functioning is important, the emphasis ideally will be placed on the identification and acceptance of sexual feelings and the development of social skills. Intellectualized, rigid, perfectionistic males with eating disorders may find it difficult to develop social relationships. Encouragement, role models, and opportunities for socialization are helpful. Premature sexual experiences may inhibit them from mature relationships and therefore should be discouraged.

Exercise. Perhaps more than with females, exercise should be a regular part of nutritional rehabilitation and weight gain. Since most males are very desirous of the development of muscle definition and wish to avoid flab, they find that the incorporation of an exercise program into treatment will give them relief from anxiety about distribution of weight and some sense of control. Exercise should be appropriate to the degree of physical distress. We begin with stretching and toning exercises and walks around the hospital ground. By the time they are ready for discharge from the hospital, they have begun a comprehensive, vigorous exercise program designed by an exercise physiologist. These programs include exercises for cardiovascular fitness, stretching, and the development of strength and muscle definition. We tell patients initially that the regaining of their weight is the first priority, and then over the next six to nine months redistribution of weight becomes a realistic possibility.

Improved Adaptation. Of fundamental importance is the development of more adaptive ways of dealing with crises in development and abnormalities in mood state by methods other than starving or binge-purge behavior. A central dynamic formulation needs to be developed for each patient, expressing the purpose the eating disorder serves in the individual's life. We therefore attempt to develop alternative methods of dealing with these issues. The goal is to make the eating disorder unnecessary, rather than to take it away.

Temperament. Most males with eating disorders are vulnerable on the basis of their temperament. An emphatic understanding of the strengths and vulnerabilities of their personality with help them make wiser choices. Obsessional individuals may learn to use thought-stopping and positive statements about themselves in situations where they normally would be inhibited. Bulimic individuals with impulsiveness learn to put some controls on their impulsivity. We develop with each patient the idea that he may be happier when he finds niches in society to which he is suited, considering the traits of his temperament. Finding a fit between personality and environment leads to less distress.

Family Issues. Finally, family issues must be addressed. These disorders cannot be blamed on any particular family constellation or function. Family treatment first of all means information, support, and the alleviation of guilt. An assessment of the family's methods of communication and styles of interaction is essential. Often the patient develops a chronic "sick" role, around which he adapts. Restoring a chronically ill person to a family requires hard work on the part of the whole family.

What Does the Future Hold?

Larger population studies will be helpful in defining the exact incidence of anorexia and bulimia. It is hoped that the studies will give both a general estimate of the incidence of these disorders and their occurrence in special groups. Genetic studies may further elucidate the reasons why particular males become vulnerable to eating disorders. A variety of treatment trials comparing different modalities in males with eating disorders will lead to better treatment methods. At present, there is no reason to consider males with eating disorders as essentially different from females except in the ways noted above. This means that the death rate and the morbidity for males will be declining, as it is for females. An optimistic attitude needs to be developed toward changing some fundamental attitudes of our society, which overemphasizes dieting behavior, rather than lifelong moderation. A society that emphasizes quick fixes, not fundamental problems, needs to be changed and can be changed by combining a reorientation of values with the results of up-to-date scientific studies.

References

Andersen, A. E., and Mickalide, A. D. "Anorexia Nervosa in the Male: An Underdiagnosed Disorder." *Psychosomatics,* 1983, *24,* 12.

Burns, T., and Crisp, A. H. "Outcome of Anorexia Nervosa in Males." *British Journal of Psychiatry*, 1984, *145*, 319-325.

Gull, W. W. "Anorexia Nervosa (Apepsia Hysterica, Anorexia Hysterica)." *Transactions of the Clinical Society of Medicine*, 1874, *7*, 22-28.

Gwirtsman, H. E., and Gerner, R. H. "Neurochemical Abnormalities in Anorexia Nervosa: Similarities to Affective Disorders." *Biological Psychiatry*, 1981, *16* (10), 991-995.

Herzog, D. B., Norman, D. K., Gordon, C., and Pepose, M. "Sexual Conflict and Eating Disorders in 27 Males." *American Journal of Psychiatry*, 1984, *141*, 8.

Keys, A., Brożek, J., Henschel, A., Mickelsen, O., and Taylor, H. L. *The Biology of Human Starvation*. Vol. 2. Minneapolis: University of Minnesota Press, 1950.

Morton, R. *Phthisiologia: Or a Treatise of Consumptions Wherein the Difference, Nature, Causes, Signs, and Cure of All Sorts of Consumptions Are Explained.* London: Sam Smith and Benjamin Walford, 1694.

Nylander, I. "The Feeling of Being Fat and Dieting in a School Population." *Acta Sociologica and Medica Scandinavica*, 1971, *1*, 17-26.

Yates, A., Leehey, K., and Shisslak, C. M. "Running: An Analogue of Anorexia?" *New England Journal of Medicine*, 1983, *308*, 5.

Arnold E. Andersen is associate professor of psychiatry and behavioral sciences at The Johns Hopkins University School of Medicine in Baltimore, Maryland.

Possible causes for obesity are examined and included as part of the spectrum of eating disorders.

The Pathogenesis and Treatment of Obesity

John S. Daniels

Obesity is the most common metabolic disorder in humans. After the age of forty years, over 60 percent of men and women in the United States are greater than 10 percent above ideal body weight, and over 30 percent of men and 40 percent of women are frankly obese, as defined here (Metropolitan Life Insurance Company, 1960). The socioeconomic consequences of this statistic are incalculable. Obese individuals are excluded from participating fully in many professions and from many cultural and social activities. Furthermore, obesity is an independent risk factor for the development of numerous debilitating illnesses, including coronary artery disease, atherosclerosis, chronic lung disease, hyperlipidemia, gallstones, degenerative joint disease, diabetes meillitus, hypertension, and a number of other less serious problems. Thus, the health care costs that result as a direct consequence of obesity are enormous.

The definition of obesity is somewhat arbitrary, since there is a continuous distribution of body weights in the general population, with no clear division between obese and thin individuals. It appears, however, that morbidity and mortality increase significantly when body weight exceeds 20 percent over ideal body weight. Thus, most authorities define obesity as that weight more than 20 percent over the ideal body weight for a given individual (Bray, 1976). Other definitions of obesity have been

F.E.F. Larocca (ed.). *Eating Disorders.*
New Directions for Mental Health Services, no. 31. San Francisco: Jossey-Bass, Fall 1986.

proposed. For example, a weight/height index (kilograms of weight divided by height in meters) emphasizes the effect of stature on weight, with obesity being defined as an index greater than 27 for men and 25 for women (Edwards and Whyte, 1962). Skin-fold thickness has also been proposed as an index for obesity, with a triceps skin-fold thickness greater than 23 mm in men and 30 mm in women being defined as obesity (Mayer, 1966). For clinical purposes, body weight is most useful. The ideal body weight for an average body build can be quickly calculated as follows: *Men:* 106 pounds for the first 5 feet in height, and 6 pounds per inch thereafter; *women:* 100 pounds for the first 5 feet in height, and five pounds per inch thereafter; for both men and women, 10 percent may be added for a large body build or 10 percent subtracted for a small body build.

Etiology

Endocrine Causes of Obesity

Classical endocrine diseases are a rare cause for obesity. Hypothyroidism has long been advocated as a common cause for obesity, as evidenced by a continuous stream of articles in the nonmedical press and by frequent prescriptions of thyroid hormone given by primary care physicians to obese patients as part of a weight-reduction program. In fact, hypothyroidism is rarely if ever responsible for the development of obesity. While it is true that the basal metabolic rate decreases by up to 30 percent in hypothyroidism, appetite also decreases, and weight gains are usually modest. Over 40 percent of hypothyroid individuals gain no weight at all (Ingbar and Woeber, 1981).

Cushing's syndrome that is secondary to hypersecretion of ACTH, adrenal adenoma, or exogenous administration of glucocorticoids, is also a rare cause for obesity. The fat distribution is distinct, involving the face, neck, trunk, and girdle areas, and it is usually accompanied by other symptoms and signs of hypercortisolism, such as purple striae, purpura, thinning of the skin, muscle wasting, hypertension, impaired glucose tolerance, and hirsutism. Cure of Cushing's syndrome almost always reverses the obese state.

Hypogonadism is also a rare cause for obesity, particularly if it occurs after puberty. Some genetic syndromes associated with hypogonadism, such as Prader-Willi syndrome (hypotonia, hypomentia, hypogonadism, and obesity), as well as other nongenetic causes of hypogonadism, including hypothalamic or pituitary tumors and primary gonadal failure, have been associated with obesity. In cases in which gonadal hormone deficiency has been clearly demonstrated, the obese state may improve with the administration of gonadal hormones.

There are several other endocrine diseases that may rarely cause obesity, including insulinoma, Stein-Leventhal syndrome, and multiple lipomatosis. The endocrine causes for obesity, however, account for less than one in five hundred cases of obesity.

Genetic Causes for Obesity

Although it has long been known that obesity is frequently a familial trait, the relative contribution of genetic versus environmental factors continues to be an issue of considerable debate.

The association of specific single-gene loci with obesity in experimental animals has been clearly shown, the best studied example being the ob/ob mutant mouse first described by Ingalls and others (1950). Single-gene loci are also associated with obesity in humans, including (1) the Laurence-Moon-Bardet-Biedl syndrome, characterized by obesity, hypogonadism, mental retardation, retinitis pigmentosa, and polydactyly (Kyriakides and others, 1981); (2) the Prader-Willi syndrome, characterized by obesity, hypotonia, hypogonadotropic hypogonadism, and mental retardation (Hofnagel, 1967); (3) the Alstrom-Hallgren syndrome, characterized by obesity, childhood blindness, nerve paralysis, and diabetes mellitus (Powers, 1980); and (4) the Morgagni-Stuart-Morel syndrome, occurring in older women and characterized by obesity, virilism, and hyperostosis (Rynearson, 1944). Although these syndromes are rare and account for only a minute fraction of the obese population, they clearly demonstrate that genetic factors can influence body weight.

The genetic factors contributing to most cases of obesity are complex and poorly understood. Numerous population studies have demonstrated that about two-thirds of obese individuals have at least one obese parent, and that one-quarter of obese individuals have two obese parents (Davenport, 1923; Dunlop and Lyon, 1931; Gurnay, 1936). Conversely, when both parents are thin, fewer than 10 percent of children are overweight. When one parent is obese, half of the children are obese, and when both parents are obese, 80 percent of offspring will be obese (Mayer, 1965). Twin studies have demonstrated that there is a greater concordance for obesity in monozygotic twins than in dizygotic twins throughout adolescence and adult life (Stunkard, 1980). Finally, adoption studies have shown concordance for obesity between adopted children and biological parents, but no concordance between adopted children and foster parents (Biron and others, 1977; Bjoreson, 1976; Withers, 1964). Thus, it does appear that genetic factors are important in the development of obesity. The mechanisms whereby these genetic factors express themselves metabolically, however, are not fully understood.

Adipocyte (Fat Cell) Hyperplasia and Hypertrophy

Knittle and Hirsch (1968) demonstrated two periods of adipocyte proliferation in nonobese children. First, within the first two years of life and, second, just prior to puberty. Subsequently, it was shown in both animals and humans that overfeeding during infancy resulted in adipocyte hyperplasia, whereas overfeeding in adulthood resulted not in hyperplasia but rather in hypertrophy of adipocytes (Knittle and others, 1979; Hager, 1977). For example, Sims and colleagues in 1973 force-fed thin adult human volunteers, achieving 20 percent to 30 percent increases in body weight. It was demonstrated in this study that the increase in adipose tissue was secondary to hypertrophy of adipocytes, without any change in adipocyte cell number (Sims and others, 1981). As a result of these and other studies, obesity has been classified into two types: *hyperplastic obesity,* characterized by severe, lifelong obesity that is anatomically generalized and resistant to therapy; and *hypertrophic obesity,* characterized by a less severe, adult-onset obesity that is more amenable to therapy (Williams, 1981). Recent evidence suggests, however, that this classification is an oversimplication.

For example, several studies have demonstrated that adult-onset obesity results not only from hypertrophy of adipocytes but also from hyperplasia of adipocytes. It appears that as the mass of adipose tissue reaches a critical mass (approximately 30 kg), there is no further increase in adipocyte size; rather, there is onset of increased numbers of adipocytes. Thus, all obese individuals have hypertrophic obesity, and as the adipose mass continues to increase, hyperplasia of adipocytes becomes the dominant controlling mechanism (Bjorntorp and Sjostrom, 1971; Bray, 1970; Hirsch and Batchelor, 1976; Hirsch and Knittle, 1970; Salans and others, 1973). Onset of obesity in infancy may in fact be associated with hypertrophy of adipocytes, without hyperplasia (Sjostrom and Bjorntorp, 1974).

Individuals with hypertrophic obesity appear better able to achieve sustained weight loss than individuals with hyperplastic obesity. In addition, while individuals may increase fat cell numbers with weight gain, no reduction in fat cell number occurs with weight reduction (Bjorntorp and Sjostrom, 1971; Bray, 1976). Thus, hyperplastic obesity may be a biological trap in which, with every increase in weight, there is a further increase in fat cell number, without any potential to reduce that number.

Setpoint Hypothesis

There is considerable evidence that, as with other body functions such as temperature, animals and humans attempt to maintain body weight at a constant level. For example, rats that are made obese by force-feeding will quickly return to their original weight when placed on an ad libitum diet (Cohn and Joseph, 1962). In the study by Sims and others (1981) human volunteers were force-fed to increase their body weight. Despite ingestion of large numbers of calories, those who did gain weight quickly returned to their baseline weights when placed on an ad libitum diet.

Conversely, obese animals and humans placed on a calorically restricted diet with resultant weight loss will quickly return to baseline weight when placed on an ad libitum diet (Johnson and Drenich, 1977); Stunkard and Penul, 1979). In fact, there have been no weight loss programs in humans that have been effective in achieving sustained weight loss, a situation that would be predicted by the setpoint hypothesis.

The mechanisms whereby body weight is maintained at a constant level are poorly understood but probably involve compensatory changes in both energy intake and energy expenditure. For example, it is typical for dieting individuals to demonstrate behavioral changes that affect food intake, including anxiety, depression, and preoccupation with food. It has also been shown that when lean individuals consume excessive numbers of calories, there is an increase in energy expenditure, exclusive of physical activity (Sims and others, 1981). Conversely, when obese individuals consume hypocaloric diets, there is a decrease in energy expenditure, exclusive of physical activity. This subject will be discussed in more detail in the next section. Suffice it to say that these weight-stabilizing mechanisms are powerful devices that maintain body weight at a "setpoint" and frustrate attempts at achieving sustained weight loss.

Pathogenesis of Obesity: Disorders of Energy Intake

Psychological and Behavioral Determinants

It is clear that cultural, social, psychological, and behavioral factors contribute to disorders of energy intake, usually resulting in obesity. For example, television advertising has had a striking impact on the eating behavior of Americans, particularly children (Lewis and Lewis, 1974; Powers and others, 1979; Stunkard, 1977). Advertisements for fast-food restaurants have resulted in fast-food items becoming some of the most frequently consumed foods in the United States. These foods are typically high in fat and calories. During weekdays, 70 percent of television food ads were devoted to high-caloric foods, whereas on weekends, 85 percent of the food ads were devoted to high-fat, high-caloric foods (Masover and Stomler, 1977). Many other social and cultural factors have been linked to the development of obesity, including childrearing practices (Mead, 1943), socioeconomic status (Goldblatt and others, 1965), urban life-style, religious background, and many practices of the food processing industry (McGovern, 1977). Stunkard (1980) makes a strong case for devoting more attention to social and environmental influences in the treatment of obesity.

One of the most widely accepted theories in the field of obesity is Schacter's externality theory (Roden, 1980). This theory proposes that obese individuals react more to external cues, such as the sight of food, than do lean individuals. In contrast, lean individuals are more stimulated to eat by internal physiological cues that regulate hunger. Thus, according to this theory, the obese person eats because it is time to eat or because the food is tempting, whereas the lean person eats because he or she is hungry. Not all studies have confirmed this difference between obese and lean individuals (Atkinson and Rinquette, 1967).

Attempts to link a psychiatric disorder or personality type to obesity have not been successful (Johnson and others, 1976; Weinberg and others, 1961). The psychoanalytic theory of obesity proposes that overeating results from a regression to the oral stage of psychosexual development. Important oral activities, such as eating, nursing, and thumbsucking, are equated in early life with intimacy and love. In later life, if the need for love and security is not satisfied, overeating may substitute for these unfulfilled needs. There is some evidence that this theory holds true for some individuals; psychoanalysis, in at least one study, has been said to be an effective form of treatment for some obese individuals (Rand and Stunkard, 1978).

Central Nervous System Determinants

Destruction of the ventromedial nucleus of the hypothalamus results in hyperphagia and obesity in animals and humans (Bray and York, 1972). Several studies have shown that lesions of the ventromedial nucleus result in increased insulin levels and lipogenesis, independent of the hyperphagia that occurs (Hustuedt and Lovo, 1972). It is now thought that the neurogenic rise in insulin secretion is primarily responsible for the obesity that occurs in this syndrome (Inoue, 1978), since excess insulin results in hyperphagia and lipogenesis. This syndrome has been rarely described in humans (Bray and Gallagher, 1975).

Lesions of the ventromedial nucleus also result in hyperreactivity of the vagus nerve, and a subdiaphragmatic vagotomy will prevent hyperphagia and obesity, following destruction of the ventromedial nucleus (McGovern, 1977). Hyperinsulinism is also prevented by vagotomy (Morley, 1980), which suggests that parasympathetic innervation of the stomach and pancreas is important in hypothalamic obesity. The relevance of this syndrome to the usual types of obesity in humans remains unclear, however.

It has long been recognized that the hypothalamus is important in the initiation of feeding and in the production of satiety. Furthermore, a number of endogenous substances may be important in appetite control, including such appetite stimulants as dopamine, alpha-agonists, and endorphins and such appetite suppressants as serotonin, beta-agonists, cholecystokinin, thyrotropin-releasing hormone, glucagon, somatotropin, glucose, and fatty acids (Powley and Opsall, 1976; Woods and others, 1981).

Recent studies have suggested an important role for the endogenous opiates, or endorphins, in producing the drive to consume food. Administration of the classic opiate, morphine, as well as a number of endogenous opiates, including beta-endorphins, met-enkephalen, and dynorphin, has been shown to induce feeding in animals and to reverse satiety induced by feeding, cholecystokinin, and thyrotropin-releasing hormone (Grandison and Guidotti, 1977; Morley and Levine, 1981, 1982). Naloxone, which is a highly specific opiate antagonist, inhibits stress-induced and starvation-induced feeding (Brown and Holtzman, 1979; Lowy and others, 1980) and has been shown to induce weight loss in man, including in some obese, hyperphagic patients with Prader-Willi syndrome (Sims and others, 1981; Kyriakides and others, 1981). Thus, the endogenous opiates may have a primary role in the regulation of food intake, but their role in the pathogenesis of obesity is highly speculative.

Disorders of Energy Expenditure

Although there has been considerable emphasis on excessive intake of food in the pathogenesis of obesity, it has become clear that disorders in energy expenditure are an important (and sometimes dominant) factor in the pathogenesis of obesity. Although there is little evidence in humans to confirm this possibility, there is good evidence in animal models of obesity. For example, the ob/ob mouse develops its obesity as a result of both hyperphagia and decreased energy expenditure. The early development of obesity in the ob/ob mouse, however, results exclusively from decreased energy expenditure, as food intake is no different from that observed in lean mice (Bray and York, 1972; Trayburn and others, 1981). Similar findings have been demonstrated in several other animal models, including the diabetic obese (db/ob) mouse (Contaldo and others, 1981) and the Zucker (fa/fa) rat (Boulange and others, 1979). In humans, it is difficult to perform valid experiments because of the marked heterogeneity of study groups and the absence of good experimental techniques for precisely measuring energy intake and energy expenditure. Nevertheless, the frequent observation that many obese individuals consume surprisingly few calories—and dietary surveys fail to show an abnormal intake of food for most obese individuals—suggests that in humans there may be a disturbance in energy expenditure that accounts at least in part for the development of obesity (Davenport, 1923).

Energy expenditure is usually divided into the following four compartments:

Basal Metabolic Rate (BMR). The BMR is the energy expenditure of an individual who is physically and mentally at rest in a thermoneutral environment twelve to eighteen hours after a meal. The BMR accounts for 50 percent to 75 percent of energy expenditure in humans (DuBois, 1954), and thus even a small decrease in BMR could result in obesity. Most animal studies demonstrate no difference in BMR between obese and lean groups. Some human studies actually demonstrate an increase BMR in obese subjects (Powers, 1980), although Miller has identified a group of obese human subjects who seem to have a lower BMR (McGovern, 1977).

Physical Activity. Physical activity accounts for about 20 percent to 30 percent of the energy expenditure for most normal individuals, although there is a wide variation. Many studies have attempted to demonstrate that obese subjects are less active than lean individuals. Certainly, the obesity in the animal models previously described cannot be accounted for on the basis of decreased physical activity. Nevertheless, several studies using motion pictures to estimate energy expenditure from physical activity have shown that obese subjects are less active than lean subjects (Bullen and others, 1964; Johnson and others, 1956). Furthermore, epidemiological studies have shown that individuals in physically strenuous occupations weigh less than those in more sedentary occupations (Mayer and others, 1956). Although such studies are suggestive that decreased physical activity results in obesity, the questions remains of whether the obesity results in decreased physical activity. It has been shown that the energy expenditure for a given amount of work is the same for obese and lean individuals, a finding that discounts an intrinsic defect in energy costs for physical activity in obese subjects (Goldman and Haisman, 1975).

Thermal Effect of Food (TEF). TEF is the energy expenditure resulting from the ingestion of food and accounts for from approximately 5 percent to 10 percent of total energy expenditure. TEF is most simply determined by calculating the rise in oxygen consumption above resting for the two or three hours following the ingestion of food. Most of this energy expenditure can be accounted for by the energy required for digestive absorption, transport, metabolism, and storage of the ingested food. A decrease in TEF could predispose to the development of obesity. At least two studies have demonstrated a defect in energy expenditure in obese subjects following the ingestion of food (Pittet and others, 1976; Stordy and others, 1977), but whether this defect is important in the pathogenesis of obesity is speculative.

Adaptive Thermogenesis. Adaptive thermogenesis is the energy expenditure that results from no useful work. Appearing as heat, it is a mechanism (at least in animals) for expending energy resulting from excessive food intake (Rothwell and Stod, 1979). It is best measured as the heat production following exposure to a cold environment or to overfeeding. Evidence has accumulated that obese animals have a decreased ability to produce heat in a cold environment and thus a decreased ability to maintain core temperatures. In fact, when ob/ob mice are placed in a temperature of less than 5°C, they rapidly die, whereas lean mice are able to maintain near normal temperatures (Davis and Mayer, 1954). At thermoneutral temperatures, the amount of energy expended by obese animals to maintain normal body temperature is half the energy required for lean animals. This decreased adaptive thermogenesis probably accounts in large part for the decreased total energy expenditure that occurs in obese animal models.

There is some evidence that obese humans have a decreased energy expenditure after exposure to a cold environment when compared to lean individuals (Jequier, 1981). There are few experiments that adequately study adaptive thermogenesis in humans; however, it is intriguing to speculate that obesity may result from a decreased capacity to increase energy expenditure in response to cold environments or in response to overfeeding.

Treatment of Obesity

A successful weight-loss program must provide the following ingredients: a proper diet; a behavior modification program with a long-term follow-up; and an exercise program, when appropriate. A variety of adjunctive agents is available and should be used as required, including anorectic drugs, various hormones, and, in extreme cases, surgical procedures.

Conclusion

At present, our understanding of the pathogenesis of obesity is in the early stages. It is certain that the causes of obesity are many and complex. The moderately overweight individual whose obesity had its onset in the fourth decade of life certainly suffers from a disorder that is quite different from that of the morbidly obese individual who has been overweight since childhood. The obese individual who consumes 4,000 calories daily is certainly different from a similarly obese individual who consumes only 1,500 calories daily. Our understanding of basic mechanisms of energy expenditure is severely limited by an inability to clinically measure the various compartments of energy expenditure in a precise way. Exciting new research in brain structure and chemistry may allow us one day to understand the controlling mechanisms of energy intake and expenditure. As we begin to understand these controlling mechanisms, more rational and successful treatments for obesity should emerge.

References

Atkinson, R. M., and Rinquette, E. L. "A Survey of Biographical and Psychological Features in Extraordinary Fatness." *Psychological Medicine*, 1967, *29*, 121-133.

Biron, P., Mongeau, J. G., and Bertrand, D. "Familial Resemblance of Body Weight and Weight/Height in 374 Homes with Adopted Children." *Journal of Pediatrics*, 1977, *91*, 555-558.

Bjoreson, M. "The Aetiology of Obesity in Children." *Acta Paediatrica Scandinavica*, 1976, *65*, 279-287.

Bjorntorp, P., and Sjostrom, L. "Number and Size of Adipose Tissue Fat Cells in Relation to Metabolism in Human Obesity." *Metabolism,* 1971, *20,* 703–713.

Boulange, A., Plancke, E., and de Gasquet, P. "Onset of Genetic Obesity in the Absence of Hyperphagia During the First Week of Life in the Zucker Rat (fa/fa)." *Journal of Lipid Research,* 1979, *20,* 859–865.

Bray, G. A. "Measurement of Subcutaneous Fat Cells from Obese Patients." *Annals of Internal Medicine,* 1970, *73,* 565–569.

Bray, G. A. *The Obese Patient.* Philadelphia: W. B. Saunders, 1976.

Bray, G. A., and Gallagher, T. F. "Manifestations of Hypothalamic Obesity in Man: A Comprehensive Investigation of Eight Patients and a Review of the Literature." *Medicine,* 1975, *54,* 301–333.

Bray, G. A., and York, D. A. "Studies on Food Intake of Genetically Obese Rats." *American Journal of Physiology,* 1972, *233,* 176–179.

Brown, D. R., and Holtzman, S. G. "Suppression of Deprivation-Induced Food and Water Intake in Rats and Mice by Naloxone." *Pharmocology of Biochemical Behavior,* 1979, *26,* 2113–2118.

Bullen, B. A., Reed, R. B., and Mayer, J. "Physical Activity of Obesity and Nonobese Adolescent Girls." *American Journal of Clinical Nutrition,* 1964, *14,* 211–233.

Cohn, C., and Joseph, D. "Influence of Body Weight and Body Fat on Appetite of 'Normal' Lean and Obese Rats." *Yale Journal of Biological Medicine,* 1962, *34,* 598–607.

Contaldo, F., Gerber, H., Coward, W. A., and Trayburn, P. "Milk Intake in Pre-Weanling Genetically Obese Mice." In G. Enzi and G. Ciepoldi (eds.), *Obesity: Pathogenesis and Treatment.* New York: Academic Press, 1981.

Davenport, C. B. *Body Build and Its Inheritance.* Publication 309. Washington, D.C.: Carnegie Institution of Washington, 1923.

Davis, T.R.A., and Mayer, J. "Imperfect Homeothermia in the Hereditary Obese-Hyperglycemic Syndrome of Mice." *American Journal of Physiology,* 1954, *177,* 222.

DuBois, E. F. "Energy Metabolism." *Annual Review of Physiology,* 1954, *16,* 125–134.

Dunlop, D. M., and Lyon, R. M. "Study of 523 Cases of Obesity." *Edinburgh Medical Journal,* 1931, *38,* 561–577.

Edwards, K.D.G., and Whyte, H. M. "The Simple Measurement of Obesity." *Clinical Science,* 1962, *22,* 347.

Goldblatt, P. B., Moore, M. E., and Stunkard, A. J. "Social Factors in Obesity." *Journal of the American Medical Association,* 1965, *192,* 1039–1044.

Goldman, R. F., and Haisman, M. E. "Experimental Obesity in Man: Metabolic Rate in Relation to Dietary Intake." In *Obesity in Perspective.* Washington, D.C.: U.S. Government Printing Office, 1975.

Grandison, S., and Guidotti, A. "Stimulation of Food Intake by Muscimol and Beta Endorphin." *Neuropharmacology,* 1977, *16,* 533–536.

Gurnay, R. "Hereditary Factors in Obesity." *Archives of Internal Medicine,* 1936, *57,* 557–561.

Hager, A. "Body Fat and Adipose Cellularity in Infants: A Longitudinal Study." *Metabolism,* 1977, *26,* 607–612.

Hirsch, J., and Batchelor, B. "Adipose Tissue Cellularity in Human Obesity." *Clinical Endocrinological Metabolism,* 1976, *5,* 299–311.

Hirsch, J., and Knittle, J. L. "Cellularity of Obese and Nonobese Human Adipose Tissue." *Federation Proceedings,* 1970, *29,* 1516–1521.

Hofnagel, R. "The Prader-Willi Syndrome." *Journal of Mental Deficiency,* 1967, *2,* 1–10.

Hustuedt, B. E., and Lovo, A. "Correlation Between Hyperinsulinism and Hyperphagia in Rats with Ventromedial Hypothalamic Lesions." *Acta Physiologica Scandinavica*, 1972, *84*, 29–34.

Ingalls, A. M., Dickie, M. M., and Snell, G. D. "Obese, New Mutation in the Mouse." *Journal of Heredity*, 1950, *41*, 317–318.

Ingbar, S. H., and Woeber, K. A. "The Thyroid Gland." In R. H. Williams (ed.), *Textbook of Endocrinology*. Philadelphia: W. B. Saunders, 1981.

Inoue, S. "Transplantation of Pancreatic Beta Cells Prevents Development of Hypothalamic Obesity in Rats." *American Journal of Physiology*, 1978, *235*, E266.

Jequier, E. "Thermogenic Regulation in Man." In G. Enzi and G. Ciepoldi (eds.), *Obesity: Pathogenesis and Treatment*. New York: Academic Press, 1981.

Johnson, D., and Drenich, E. J. "Therapeutic Fasting in Morbid Obesity: Long-Term Follow-Up." *Archives of Internal Medicine*, 1977, *137*, 1381–1382.

Johnson, M. L., Burke, B. S., and Mayer, J. "The Prevalence and Incidence of Obesity in a Cross-Section of Elementary and Secondary School Children." *American Journal of Clinical Nutrition*, 1956, *4*, 231–238.

Johnson, S. F., Swenson, W. M., and Gastineau, C. F. "Personality Characteristics in Obesity: Relation of MMPI Profile and Age of Onset of Obesity in Success in Weight Reduction." *American Journal of Clinical Nutrition*, 1976, *29*, 626–632.

Knittle, J. L., and Hirsch, J. "Effect of Early Nutrition on the Development of Fat Epididymal Fat Pads: Cellulosity and Metabolism" *Journal of Clinical Investigation*, 1968, *47*, 2091.

Knittle, J. L., and Hirsch, J. "Effect of Early Nutrition on the Development of Fat Epididymal Fat Pads: Cellulosity and Metabolism." *Journal of Clinical Investigation*, 1968, *47*, 2091.

Kyriakides, M., Silverstone, T., Jeffcoate, W., and Laurance, B. "Effect of Naloxone on Hyperphagia in Prader-Willi Syndrome." *Lancet*, 1981, *1*, 876–877.

Lewis, C. E., and Lewis, M. A. "The Impact of Television Commercials on Health-Related Beliefs and Behavior of Children." *Pediatrics*, 1974, *53*, 431–435.

Lowy, M. T., Marchel, R. P., and Yim, G.K.W. "Naloxone Reduction of Stress-Related Feeding." *Life Sciences*, 1980, *26*, 2113–2118.

McGovern, G. *Dietary Goals for the United States*. Washington, D.C.: U.S. Government Printing Office, 1977.

Masover, L., and Stomler, J. Presentation to the 1976 convention of the American Public Health Association. In G. McGovern (ed.), *Dietary Goals for the United States*. (2nd ed.) Washington, D.C.: U.S. Government Printing Office, 1977.

Mayer, J. "Genetic Factors in Human Obesity." *Annals of the New York Academy of Sciences*, 1965, *131*, 412.

Mayer, J. "Some Aspects of the Problem of Regulation of Food Intake and Obesity." *New England Journal of Medicine*, 1966, *274*, 610.

Mayer, J., Roy, P., and Mitra, K. P. "Relation Between Caloric Intake, Body Weight, and Physical Work: Studies in an Industrial Male Population in West Bengal." *American Journal of Clinical Nutrition*, 1956, *4*, 169–175.

Mead, M. "Dietary Pattern and Food Habits." *Journal of the American Dietetic Association*, 1943, *19*, 1–5.

Metropolitan Life Insurance Company. "Frequency of Overweight and Underweight." *Statistical Bulletin*, 1960, *41*, 4.

Morley, J. E. "The Neuroendocrine Control of Appetite." *Life Science*, 1980, *27*, 355–368.

Morley, J. E., and Levine, A. S. "Dynorphin (1-13) Induces Spontaneous Feeding in Rats." *Life Science*, 1981, *18*, 1901–1903.

Morley, J. E., and Levine, A. S. "The Role of Endogenous Opiates on Regulation of Appetite." *American Journal of Clinical Nutrition*, 1982, *35*, 757–761.

Pittet, P., Chappius, P., and Acheson, K. "Thermic Effect of Glucose on Obese Subjects Studied by Direct and Indirect Calorimetry." *British Journal of Nutrition*, 1976, *35*, 281.

Powers, P. S. *Obesity: The Regulation of Weight.* Baltimore: Williams & Wilkins, 1980.

Powers, P. S., Younger, D., and Fernandez, R. "Television Advertising and Children's Food Preferences." Paper submitted to second regional congress of the American Association of Social Psychiatry, Louisville, Kentucky, 1979.

Powley, T. L., and Opsall, C. A. "Autonomic Changes of the Hypothalamus Feeding Syndrome." In D. Novin (ed.), *Hunger: Basic Mechanisms and Clinical Implications.* New York: Raven Press, 1976.

Rand, C. S., and Stunkard, A. J. "Obesity and Psychoanalysis." *American Journal of Psychiatry*, 1978, *135*, 547–551.

Roden, J. "The Externality Theory Today in Obesity." In A. J. Stunkard (ed.), *Obesity.* Philadelphia: W. B. Saunders, 1980.

Rothwell, M. J., and Stod, M. J. "Role for Brown Adipose Tissue in Diet Induced Thermogenesis." *Nature*, 1979, *281*, 31–35.

Rynearson, E. H. "The Problems of Obesity." *Proceedings of the Institute of Medical Changes*, 1944, *15*, 35.

Salans, L. B., Cushman, S. W., and Weissman, R. E. "Studies on Human Adipose Tissue: Adipose Cell Size and Number of Nonobese and Obese Patients." *Journal of Clinical Investigation*, 1973, *52*, 929–941.

Sims, E.A.H., Danforth, E., Morton, E. S., Bray, G. A., Glennon, J. A., and Salans, L. B. "Endocrine and Metabolic Effects of Experimental Obesity in Man." *Recent Progress in Hormonal Research*, 1981, *29*, 457.

Sjostrom, L., and Bjorntorp, P. "Body Composition and Adipose Tissue Cellularity in Human Obesity." *Acta Medica Scandinavica*, 1974, *195*, 201–211.

Stordy, B. J., Marks, V., Kalucy, R. S., Path, R. S., and Crisp, A. H. "Weight Gain, Thermic Effect of Glucose and Resting Metabolism Rate During Recovery from Anorexia Nervosa." *American Journal of Clinical Nutrition*, 1977, *30*, 138–146.

Stunkard, A. J. "Obesity in the Social Environment: Current Status, Future Prospects." *Annals of the New York Academy of Sciences*, 1977, *300*, 298–320.

Stunkard, A. J. "The Social Environment and the Control of Obesity." In A. J. Stunkard (ed.), *Obesity.* Philadelphia: W. B. Saunders, 1980.

Stunkard, A. J., and Penul, S. B. "Behavior Modification in the Treatment of Obesity: The Problem of Maintaining Weight Loss." *Archives of General Psychiatry*, 1979, *36*, 801–806.

Trayburn, P., Thurlby, P. L., Goodbody, A. E., and James, W.P.T. "Brown Adipose Tissue and Thermogenesis in Obesity." In G. Enzi and G. Ciepoldi (eds.), *Obesity: Pathogenesis and Treatment.* New York: Academic Press, 1981.

Weinberg, N., Mendelsoh, M., and Stunkard, A. J. "A Failure to Find Distinctive Personality Features in a Group of Obese Men." *American Journal of Psychiatry*, 1961, *117*, 1035–1037.

Williams, R. H. *Textbook of Endocrinology.* (6th ed.) Philadelphia: W. B. Saunders, 1981.

Withers, R.F.J. "Problems in the Genetics of Human Obesity." *Eugenics Review*, 1964, *56*, 81–90.

Woods, S. C., West, D. B., Stein, L. J., McKay, L. D., Lotter, E. C., Porte, S. G., Kenney, N. J., and Porte, D. "Peptides and Control of Meal Size." *Diabetologia*, 1981, *20*, 305–313.

John S. Daniels is assistant clinical professor of medicine at the Washington University School of Medicine in St. Louis, Missouri.

The treatment of Anorexia Nervosa and bulimia through the use of pharmacological approaches is described, using a variety of case studies.

Pharmacological Approaches to the Treatment of Eating Disorders

W. J. Kenneth Rockwell

There has always been interest in pharmacological and other somatic treatments of Anorexia Nervosa and disorders related to it, but in the United States, at least, such interest languished for over thirty years after the publication of Waller and others' (1940) psychoanalytic formulation. The writings of Hilde Bruch (1962, 1965, 1973), however, began to gain ascendancy. She stressed the need for immediate attention to the nutritional status of anorectic patients and to perceptions, attitudes, and behaviors associated with ingestion. Her persistence led to a major shift in the conceptualization and treatment of eating disorders and brought on the present epoch in the field.

Such changes, coupled with concomitant increased interest in developing pharmacological approaches to psychiatric illnesses in general, have led to renewed attempts at drug treatments for eating disorders. This chapter will not contain a comprehensive review of drug treatments over time; for a review of the older literature, see Bliss and Branch (1960). Furthermore, much of the material covered herein has been reviewed previously (Johnson and others, 1983; Rockwell and others, 1984; Gwirtsman and others, 1984). This chapter will review drug treatments of anorexia and bulimia, with the focus on controlled drug trials.

F.E.F. Larocca (ed.). *Eating Disorders.*
New Directions for Mental Health Services, no. 31. San Francisco: Jossey-Bass, Fall 1986.

Anorexia Nervosa

Any one of three clinical effects of medication, including hormonal preparations, is useful in the treatment of Anorexia Nervosa. The first effect is weight gain through metabolic mechanisms. The second is assistance by whatever means in weight maintenance once weight has been restored to a proper level. The third and most widely hoped for effect of psychoactive medications is facilitation of a change in attitude. This can be sought through the dissipation of a body-image delusion, elimination of a phobic fear of fatness or of anxiety about the effects of introducing food into the body, or interruption of obsessive-compulsive processes related to the pursuit of thinness. Changes in mood have also been sought, on the assumption that the basic defect might be an underlying depression, with concomitant loss of appetite, social withdrawal, and suicidal impulses. It is felt that without attitudinal, behavioral, or mood changes, the first two beneficial effects would be limited in that eventually patients would discontinue their medication, with a resultant decline in weight.

A variety of agents—with plausible rationales given for their use— has been reported to be effective in open trials. Usually the number of patients has been small, and weight gain has been the criterion for success. The drug trials reported below are double-blind and placebo-controlled, except as noted. The word *significant* means "statistically significant."

Neuroleptics. Because of anecdotal reports of at least limited success with neuroleptics, and because of the hypothesis of Barry and Klawans (1976) that some major features of anorexia might be caused by cerebral dopaminergic hyperfunction, the use of neuroleptics was investigated.

Vandereycken (1984) reported a study using the selective dopamine antagonist sulpiride. Eighteen female patients participated in two medication periods of three weeks each, alternating sulpiride and placebo, or the reverse. Doses were 300 mg per day for thirteen patients, and 400 mg per day for five patients. Several measures of behavioral and attitudinal characteristics were assessed, as well as mean daily weight change, after a baseline period of one week and at the end of each medication period. Other aspects of the treatment program were similar to the one used in the pimozide study. With respect to weight increase, sulpiride at 300 mg per day was "practically always superior to placebo, especially in the first treatment period" (p. 290), but in the crossover analysis the effects did not reach significance. No direct effect of sulpiride could be established on the behavioral and attitudinal variables. The author notes that treatment without medication was efficient enough to restore weight, and that it is more important to change the weight phobia and distorted attitudes toward the body.

Tricyclic Antidepressants. Clinicians were successfully treating depressive symptoms in some anorectics, and the weight-promoting potential of tricyclics was being investigated (Paykel and others, 1973) even before the publication of family history studies showing a possible relationship between affective disorders and anorexia. Using clomipramine, Lacey and Crisp (1980) reported on two groups of eight patients, each of whom were given 50 mg of the medication or an identical placebo at bedtime from the evening following admission until target weight was reached. Patients were kept in or on their beds until obtaining target weight, were closely supervised, and were given regular individual psychotherapy. The rate of weight gain was 0.17 kg per day for the medication group, and 0.21 kg per day for the placebo group. The result occurred despite the finding that hunger—as measured by analogue scales—was significantly greater in the clomipramine groups during the first two months. On follow-up from three to nineteen months, there was a tendency after leaving the trial for the clomipramine group to maintain body weight better than the placebo group. This last finding is basically unexplained.

Biederman and others (1985) reported a study comparing the effects of amitriptyline and placebo on weight gain and a variety of other measures of psychiatric symptomatology, including depression, eating attitudes, and obsessive-compulsive tendency. Amitriptyline dosage was 3 mg/kg per day, with a maximum dosage of 175 mg per day unless adverse effects developed. Weight and change scores on various rating instruments were measured over a five-week period. No significant differences favoring amitriptyline were found in any of the outcome variables. More specifically, drug-treated patients did not show a reduction in depressive symptoms. They did encounter a substantially higher incidence of adverse effects, however. In general, none showed much improvement during the five-week period. After considering a variety of factors that might have contributed to the negative results, the authors concluded that the data did not suggest a therapeutic role for amitriptyline in the short-term treatment of anorectic patients.

Lithium Carbonate. The possible association of anorexia with affective disorders provides a rationale for lithium carbonate's use in the treatment of anorexia. In a four-week trial, Gross and others (1981) compared eight patients given lithium carbonate with eight patients given placebos. All patients participated simultaneously in a behavior modification treatment program. Steady-state levels of plasma lithium were maintained in the range of 0.9–1.4 mEq/L. Patients on lithium gained 6.8 ± 0.1 kg during the medication trial. Patients on placebo gained 5.2 ± 0.1 kg under identical study conditions. Thus, the actual increment in weight increase was small for the drug-treated group, but the analysis revealed a significant weight increase in the drug-treated group in weeks three and four, a time consistent with clinical effectiveness of lithium carbonate in the treatment of affective illnesses. With respect to attitudinal changes, the lithium-treated group showed significantly less denial or minimization of their illness, somatization, depression, obsessive-compulsive symptomatology, and fewer physical problems or feelings of being bloated or sickened by food. The authors warned strongly about the possible dangers of treatment with lithium carbonate in patients subject to hypokalemia.

Bulimia

Bulimia has emerged as a separate disease entity only in the past few years (Russell, 1979; Huon and Brown, 1984), yet a thrust in the medication treatment of it has developed rapidly. A current hypothesis is that an affective disorder underlies bulimia. Thus, it is now being treated with drugs used to treat affective disorders: tricyclic antidepressants, monoamine oxidase inhibitors, lithium carbonate, and carbamazepine. Dysphoric feelings are certainly ubiquitous among bulimics, with depression identified in a number of studies.

There have been a number of reports of beneficial effects from medications administered in open trials, including diphenylhydantoin (Green and Rau, 1974) and lithium carbonate (Hsu, 1984), as well as antidepressants (Rich, 1978; Pope and Hudson, 1982; Shader and Greenblatt, 1982; Walsh and others, 1982; Jonas and others, 1983). In a double-blind crossover trial with carbamazepine, one of six patients with bulimia improved dramatically (Kaplan and others, 1983). Again, the studies reviewed here are double-blind and placebo-controlled, unless otherwise specified.

Antidepressants. Nineteen of twenty-two female outpatients completed a six-week trial of imipramine (nine subjects) pitted against placebo (ten subjects) (Pope and others, 1983). During the treatment phase, subjects were rated every other week on the Hamilton depression scale and for binge frequency. They also rated themselves on four subjective scales. After the six-week study period, all subjects were offered continued treatment on antidepressant medication. In terms of binge frequency, the results favored the imipramine-treated group significantly: These subjects showed a 70 percent reduction in bingeing, as compared with almost no change in the placebo group. Only one drug-treated patient failed to reduce bingeing to any extent.

There was also a significant difference between the two groups on three of four of the subject-rated scales. Likewise, the mean decline in Hamilton scale scores was significantly greater for the drug-treated group, and among all subjects there was a significant positive correlation between decline in Hamilton scale scores and decrease in bingeing frequency.

On follow-up at one to eight months, twenty to twenty-two original subjects had received complete trials of antidepressant medication. Of these, eighteen (90 percent) showed moderate to marked diminution in binge-eating.

Of eighty subjects originally screened in another program of treatment for bulimia, twenty were able to complete a trial of at least two weeks on 60 mg per day of phenelzine or placebo, nine in the former group and eleven in the latter (Walsh and others, 1984).

This study began with a two-week single-blind placebo washout period, followed by eight weeks of treatment with placebo or phenelzine, the dose of which was adjusted upward to 60 mg per day by the end of week two and ultimately to as much as 90 mg per day by the end of week six for nonresponders. Patients were seen weekly, at which time data were collected from a daily binge diary kept by the patient. Two physician-rated scales and one subject-rated scale were also completed weekly.

At termination, the mean binge frequency was 2.6 per week for the phenelzine-treated group and 10.5 per week for the placebo-treated group, a significant difference. Five of the nine phenelzine-treated patients had stopped bingeing altogether, and the other four reduced their bingeing by at least 50 percent, but none of the eleven placebo-treated patients had stopped bingeing, and two of the eleven had reduced bingeing by 50 percent or more. The physician-rated Clinical Global Impression and the subject-rated Eating Attitudes Test scores at termination showed significant improvement in the drug-treated group. Hamilton rating scale scores for depression were not significantly different between the two groups until five somatic symptoms that could be side effects of phenelzine treatment were omitted and the data were reanalyzed, at which point there was found to be a significant difference in favor of the phenelzine-treated group.

In discussing the findings, the authors felt that although both drug-treated group results were favorable, and similar in this study to that of Pope and others (1983) using imipramine, the results shown with individual patients during both studies and their follow-ups suggested that monoamine oxidase inhibitors (MAOIs) may be more effective than tricyclic antidepressants in the treatment of bulimia.

In addressing the issue of the relationship between bulimia and depression, the authors noted that two of the five patients who had had complete remission of binge-eating while on phenelzine were not considered to be substantially depressed at the time treatment began. They suggested the hypothesis that bulimic patients are more likely to suffer from persistent dysphoric feelings, with feelings of tension triggering binges, and that a type of anxious depression—for which MAOIs have been particularly effective—may be more related to bulimia.

Discussion

In a review of the pharmacotherapy of eating disorders thus far, the most striking finding is the consistently meager results with the use of various medications in Anorexia Nervosa and, more recently, the consistent success reported with the use of antidepressants in bulimia. On clinical grounds alone, this should provide continued impetus to the task of identifying subgroups of eating-disordered patients who might be treated differentially, pharmacologically or otherwise. At the same time, there remains every justification for continuing the search for new pharmacological approaches to eating-disordered patients who are currently refractory to drug treatment.

In the treatment of anorexia, drugs are at present only an adjunct; weight gain per se can almost always be accomplished without them. Nevertheless, there is still the need for a medication that will enable a patient to eat normally, without terror, in order either to restore lost weight or to maintain proper weight after nutritional rehabilitation. So far, what appears to have been achieved with the use of drugs in the treatment of anorexia has been in some cases the alleviation of concomitant depression by the use of antidepressants and, with anxiolytics and neuroleptics, a modest reduction in the anxiety associated with attempts at weight gain (or maintenance). Crisp (1983) has summarized thus: "Judicious use of small doses of phenothiazines or benzodiazepines during the process of gaining weight is the best guideline currently offered for treatment" (p. 857).

Antidepressant medication has established a place in the treatment of bulimia over a short-term period. Longer-term follow-up studies are needed to assess the effects over a greater time spectrum. Among the reports supportive of a relationship between eating disorders and affective disorders are studies of patients (Cantwell and others, 1977; Strober, 1981; Johnson and Larson, 1982; Hudson and others, 1983b; Herzog, 1984; Piran and others, 1985; Walsh and others, 1985a), family histories (Winokur and others, 1980; Hudson and others, 1982, 1983a; Gershon and others, 1984; Rivinus and others, 1984), and biological markers (Gwirtsman and Gerner, 1981; Katz and others, 1984).

The matter is more complex when the attempt is made to separate eating disorders from affective disorders, since there is no dispute that many patients with anorexia and/or bulimia are depressed. In fact, depressed mood is explicit in the DSM-III criteria for bulimia. One follow-up study of depression in bulimia found a relationship between these two entities, but not such as to support the hypothesis that bulimia is a variant of affective disorder (Swift and others, 1985). In another study, the depressive symptoms were felt to be secondary to the bulimia nervosa (Johnson-Sabine and others, 1984). Still another patient study (Wold, 1983) favored the concept of severe bulimia as a symptom of major affective disorder, but not so far restricting Anorexia Nervosa. One family study of normal-weight bulimics found no difference in the prevalence of affective disorder in the relatives of patient and control probands (Stern and others, 1984). Sleep disturbances in anorectics and bulimics have been found to differ from those of patients with major depressive illnesses (Walsh and others,

1985b); and in another study, platelet MAO activity in depressed anorectics was low, as compared with that in nondepressed anorectics and controls (Biederman and others, 1985).

A review of extant studies and a summation of their findings would require another chapter. Most investigators detect a relationship between eating disorders and affective disorders. Altshuler and Weiner (1985) have addressed these issues cogently.

Antidepressants may one day be seen as a major modality in the treatment of a substantial percentage of bulimic patients, although the dangers of MAOIs will limit their use (Fairburn and Cooper, 1983). Antidepressants cannot be viewed as the sole modality for the treatment of any patient. For patients who do not respond to antidepressants, there is every justification for the continued search for a better pharmacological approach: Just as in Anorexia Nervosa, treatment remains, for the most part, lengthy, complicated, emotionally and financially expensive, and uncertain.

References

Altshuler, K. Z., and Weiner, M. F. "Anorexia Nervosa and Depression: A Dissenting View." *American Journal of Psychiatry*, 1985, *142* (3), 328–332.

Barry, V. C., and Klawans, H. L. "On the Role of Dopamine in the Pathophysiology of Anorexia Nervosa." *Journal of Neural Transmission*, 1976, *38*, 107–122.

Biederman, J., Herzog, D. B., Rivinus, T. M., Harper, G. P., Ferber, R. A., Rosenbaum, J. F., Harmatz, J. S., Tondorf, R., Orsulak, P. J., and Schildkraut, J. J. "Amitriptyline in the Treatment of Anorexia Nervosa: A Double-Blind, Placebo-Controlled Study." *Journal of Clinical Psychopharmacology*, 1985, *5* (1), 10–16.

Bliss, E. L., and Branch, C.H.H. *Anorexia Nervosa: Its History, Psychology and Biology.* New York: Hoeber, 1960.

Bruch, H. "Anorexia Nervosa and Its Differential Diagnosis." *Journal of Nervous and Mental Disorders*, 1965, *141*, 555–566.

Bruch, H. "Anorexia Nervosa and Its Differential Diagnosis." *Journal of Nervous and Mental Disorders*, 1965, 141, 555–566.

Bruch, H. *Eating Disorders: Obesity, Anorexia Nervosa, and the Person Within.* New York: Basic Books, 1973.

Cantwell, D. P., Sturzenberger, S., Burroughs, J., Salkin, B., and Green, J. K. "Anorexia Nervosa: An Affective Disorder?" *Archives of General Psychiatry*, 1977, *34*, 1087–1093.

Crisp, A. H. "Anorexia Nervosa." *British Medical Journal*, 1983, *287*, 855–858.

Fairburn, C. G., and Cooper, P. J. "MAOIs in the Treatment of Bulimia." *American Journal of Psychiatry*, 1983, *140* (7), 949–950.

Gershon, E. S., Schreiber, J. L., Hamovit, J. R., Dibble, E. D., Kaye, W., Nurnberger, J. I., Jr., Andersen, A. E., and Ebert, M. H. "Clinical Findings on Patients with Anorexia Nervosa and Affective Illness in Their Relatives." *American Journal of Psychiatry*, 1984, *141*, 1419–1422.

Green, R. S., and Rau, J. H. "Treatment of Compulsive Eating Disturbances with Anti-Convulsant Medication." *American Journal of Psychiatry*, 1974, *131*, 428–432.

Gross, H. A., Ebert, M. H., Faden, V. B., Goldberg, S. C., Nee, L. E., and Kaye, W. H. "A Double-Blind Controlled Trial of Lithium Carbonate in Primary Anorexia Nervosa." *Journal of Clinical Psychopharmacology*, 1981, *1* (6), 376–381.

Gwirtsman, H. E., and Gerner, R. H. "Neurochemical Abnormalities in Anorexia Nervosa: Similarities to Affective Disorders." *Biological Psychiatry*, 1981, *16* (10), 991–995.

Gwirtsman, H. E., Kaye, W., Weintraub, M., and Jimerson, D. C. "Pharmacologic Treatment of Eating Disorders." *Psychiatric Clinics of North America*, 1984, 7 (4), 863–878.

Herzog, D. B. "Are Anorexic and Bulimic Patients Depressed?" *American Journal of Psychiatry*, 1984, *141*, 1594–1597.

Hsu, L.K.G. "Treatment of Bulimia with Lithium." *American Journal of Psychiatry*, 1984, *141* (10), 1260–1262.

Hudson, J. I., Laffer, P. S., and Pope, H. G., Jr. "Bulimia Related to Affective Disorder by Family History and Response to Dexamethasone Suppression Test." *American Journal of Psychiatry*, 1982, *139*, 685–687.

Hudson, J. I., Pope, H. G., Jr., Jonas, J. M., and Yurgelun-Todd, D. "Family History Study of Anorexia Nervosa and Bulimia." *British Journal of Psychiatry*, 1983a, *142*, 133–138.

Hudson, J. I., Pope, H. G., Jr., Jonas, J. M., and Yurgelun-Todd, D. "Phenomenologic Relationship of Eating Disorders to Major Affective Disorder." *Psychiatry Research*, 1983b, *9*, 345–354.

Huon, G. F., and Brown, L. B. "Bulimia: The Emergence of a Syndrome." *Australian and New Zealand Journal of Psychiatry*, 1984, *18*, 113–126.

Johnson, C., and Larson, R. "Bulimia: An Analysis of Moods and Behavior." *Psychosomatic Medicine*, 1982, *44*, 341–351.

Johnson, C., Stuckey, M., and Mitchell, J. E. "Psychopharmacological Treatment of Anorexia Nervosa and Bulimia: Review and Synthesis." *The Journal of Nervous and Mental Disease*, 1983, *171* (9), 524–538.

Johnson-Sabine, E. C., Wood, K. H., and Wakeling, A. "Mood Changes in Bulimia Nervosa." *British Journal of Psychiatry*, 1984, *145*, 512–516.

Jonas, J. M., Pope, H. G., Jr., and Hudson, J. I. "Treatment of Bulimia with MAOIs." *Journal of Clinical Psychopharmacology*, 1983, *3*, 59–60.

Kaplan, A. S., Garfinkel, P. E., Darby, P. L., and Garner, D. M. "Carbamazepine in the Treatment of Bulimia." *American Journal of Psychiatry*, 1983, *140* (9), 1225–1226.

Katz, J. L., Kuperberg, A., Pollack, C. P., Walsh, B. T., Zumoff, B., and Weiner, H. "Is There a Relationship Between Eating Disorder and Affective Disorder? New Evidence from Sleep Recordings." *American Journal of Psychiatry*, 1984, *141* (6), 753–759.

Lacey, J. H., and Crisp, A. H. "Hunger, Food Intake and Weight: The Impact of Clomipramine on Refeeding Anorexia Nervosa Populations." *Postgraduate Medical Journal*, 1980, *56* (1), 79–85.

Paykel, E. S., Mueller, P. S., and de la Vergne, P. M. "Amitriptyline, Weight Gain and Carbohydrate Craving: A Side Effect." *British Journal of Psychiatry*, 1973, *123*, 501–507.

Piran, N., Kennedy, S., Garfinkel, P. E., and Owens, M. "Affective Disturbance in Eating Disorders." *The Journal of Nervous and Mental Disease*, 1985, *173* (7), 395–400.

Pope, H. G., and Hudson, J. I. "Treatment of Bulimia with Antidepressants." *Psychopharmacology*, 1982, *78*, 167–179.

Pope, H. G., Jr., Hudson, J. I., Jonas, J. M., and Yurgelun-Todd, D. "Bulimia Treated with Imipramine: A Placebo-Controlled, Double-Blind Study." *American Journal of Psychiatry*, 1983, *140* (5), 554–558.

Rich, C. L. "Self-Induced Vomiting: Psychiatric Considerations." *Journal of the American Medical Association*, 1978, *239*, 2688–2689.

Rivinus, T. M., Biederman, J., Herzog, D. B., Kemper, K., Harper, G. P., Harmatz, J. S., and Houseworth, S. "Anorexia Nervosa and Affective Disorders: A Controlled Family History Study." *American Journal of Psychiatry*, 1984, *141* (11), 1414-1418.

Rockwell, W.J.K., Nishita, J. K., and Ellinwood, E. H., Jr. "Anorexia Nervosa: Current Perspectives in Research." *Psychiatric Clinics of North America*, 1984, 7 (2), 223-233.

Russell, G. "Bulimia Nervosa: An Ominous Variant of Anorexia Nervosa." *Psychological Medicine*, 1979, *9* (3), 429-448.

Shader, R. I., and Greenblatt, D. J. "The Psychiatrist as Mind Sweeper." *Journal of Clinical Psychopharmacology*, 1982, *2*, 233-234.

Stern, S. L., Dixon, K. N., Nemzer, E., Lake, M. D., Sansone, R. A., Smeltzer, D. J., Lantz, S., and Schrier, S. S. "Affective Disorder in the Families of Women with Normal-Weight Bulimia." *American Journal of Psychiatry*, 1984, *141* (10), 1224-1227.

Strober, M. "The Significance of Bulimia in Juvenile Anorexia Nervosa: An Exploration of Possible Etiological Factors." *International Journal of Eating Disorders*, 1981, *1*, 28-43.

Swift, W. J., Kalin, N. H., Wamboldt, F. S., Kaslow, N., and Ritholz, M. "Depression in Bulimia at 2- to 5-Year Follow-Up." *Psychiatric Research*, 1985, *14*, 38-46.

Vandereycken, W. "Neuroleptics in the Short-Term Treatment of Anorexia Nervosa: A Double-Blind Placebo-Controlled Study with Sulpiride." *British Journal of Psychiatry*, 1984, *144*, 288-292.

Waller, J. V., Kaufman, M. R., and Deutsch, F. "Anorexia Nervosa: A Psychosomatic Entity." *Psychosomatic Medicine*, 1940, *2*, 3-16.

Walsh, B. T., Goetz, R., Roose, S. P., Fingeroth, S., and Glassman, A. H. "EEG-Monitored Sleep in Anorexia Nervosa and Bulimia." *Biological Psychiatry*, 1985b, *20*, 947-956.

Walsh, B. T., Roose, S. P., Glassman, A. H., Gladis, M., and Sadik, C. "Bulimia and Depression." *Psychosomatic Medicine*, 1985a, *47* (2), 123-131.

Walsh, B. T., Stewart, J. W., Roose, S. P., Gladis, M., and Glassman, A. H. "Treatment of Bulimia with Phenelzine: A Double-Blind, Placebo-Controlled Study." *Archives of General Psychiatry*, 1984, *41*, 1105-1110.

Walsh, B. T., Stewart, J. W., Wright, L., Harrison, W., Roose, S. P., and Glassman, A. H. "Treatment of Bulimia with Monoamine Oxidase Inhibitors." *American Journal of Psychiatry*, 1982, *139* (12), 1629-1630.

Winokur, A., March, V., and Mendels, J. "Primary Affective Disorder in Relatives of Patients with Anorexia Nervosa." *American Journal of Psychiatry*, 1980, *137* (6), 695-698.

Wold, P. N. "Anorexic Syndromes and Affective Disorder." *The Psychiatric Journal of the University of Ottawa*, 1983, *8* (3), 116-119.

W. J. Kenneth Rockwell is assistant professor of psychiatry and director, Anorexia Nervosa/Bulimia Treatment Program, at Duke University Medical Center in Durham, North Carolina.

*Several methodologically sound studies support the efficacy of
antidepressant medications for the treatment of bulimia.
Various forms of psychotherapy—particularly cognitive
behavioral and group therapy—also appear to be promising
treatments but have not yet been adequately assessed in
well-designed controlled studies.*

Treatment of Bulimia:
A Review of Current Studies

James I. Hudson, Harrison G. Pope, Jr.

Numerous theories have been proposed to explain the etiology of bulimia.
Thus, it is hardly surprising that a wide range of therapeutic techniques
has been used in an attempt to treat it. Unfortunately, few of these
approaches have been formally assessed for their efficacy. This chapter
reviews critically the published studies of treatment of bulimia. For tech-
nical details of the various treatments, the reader is referred to other
chapters of this volume describing the specific therapies.

Psychosocial Treatments

Psychodynamic and Family Therapy. Although psychodynamic
treatments are probably the most widely prescribed therapy for patients
with bulimia, they are also the least well conceptualized in the literature
and the least studied. There is, to date, no available published clinical
series reporting the effect of individual psychodynamic psychotherapy in
bulimic patients.

Family therapy—based on hypotheses implicating family patterns
in the genesis of eating disorders—is also occasionally used to treat bulimia. Only one group, Schwartz and colleagues, however, has actually published its experience with this approach (Schwartz, 1982; Schwartz and

F.E.F. Larocca (ed.). *Eating Disorders.*
New Directions for Mental Health Services, no. 31. San Francisco: Jossey-Bass, Fall 1986.

others, 1985). Employing a largely psychodynamic framework with some behavioral elements, the authors treated thirty consecutive bulimic patients with family therapy (Schwartz and others, 1985). All patients began with greater than five binge-eating episodes per week. Treatment consisted of between two and ninety sessions, with an average of twenty-seven. At the end of treatment (defined as being seen less than once monthly), 66 percent of patients had fewer than two bingeing episodes per month, and 10 percent had fewer than two episodes per week. Follow-up data were obtained from one to forty-two months after treatment. All patients who had fewer than two bingeing episodes per month at the end of treatment had maintained their improvement, whereas two of the three who were bingeing once or twice monthly had worsened.

Pending a full exposition of these results, which are to appear in a book, several aspects of the study make its interpretation difficult. First, not all patients actually received family therapy: Some were seen in individual therapy, with an emphasis on family dynamics, and some were seen with friends. The family members involved were not always parents or siblings but were sometimes the "families of procreation," including spouses and children. Second, the number of sessions was not prescribed in advance, and the wide range—from two to ninety sessions—suggests that those receiving a small number of sessions may have been given a type of therapy different from the therapy of those receiving a large number of sessions. Third, the selection procedure (particularly the inclusion and exclusion criteria) was not specified, nor did the authors describe how they handled dropouts. Clearly, if a number of patients left treatment prematurely but were not scored in the final results, the findings in the thirty "completed" patients may have been too optimistic. Fourth, the authors have presented their treatment as one that evolved during the period of study. Thus, this study was not prospective, in the sense that a set of procedures derived from pilot data was employed; rather, it was (and is) a retrospective review of some of the authors' experience with this treatment modality, with the design of treatment following the exigencies of clinical practice, rather than a formalized research protocol. Fifth, the observations were uncontrolled, and outcome was evaluated on a nonblind basis.

Given their encouraging preliminary results, however, it is hoped that the authors will initiate a formal study of bulimia, applying a uniform family therapy technique. Ideally, such a study would be controlled—using, say, individual psychodynamic psychotherapy for comparison.

Behavior Therapy. Several behavioral models of bulimia have appeared, variously conceptualizing bulimic symptoms as maintained by dieting behavior, stressful antecedents, the anxiety-reducing property of self-induced vomiting, or dysfunctional cognitions regarding shape and weight. Treatments have been developed that aim to eliminate the bulimic symptoms either directly, by positive reinforcement of abstinence from bulimic symptoms, or indirectly, by modifying one or more of the proposed reinforcers cited above.

The literature on the effects of individual behavior therapy in bulimia consists largely of reports of successful treatment involving either a single case or a small series (fewer than six patients: Kenny and Solyom, 1971; Monti and others, 1977; Welch, 1979; Linden, 1980; Grinc, 1982; Long and Cordle, 1982; Rosen and Leitenberg, 1982; Mizes and Lohr, 1983; Leitenberg and others, 1984). Two larger uncontrolled series of patients have been reported, both using cognitive behavioral therapy (Fairburn, 1981; Ordman and Kirschenbaum, 1985).

Fairburn (1981) prospectively treated eleven bulimic women with behavioral and cognitive techniques, described in detail elsewhere (Fairburn, 1985). Nine of the eleven patients stopped bingeing after three to twelve months of treatment. The duration of treatment was five to eight months in nine patients: One patient dropped out after three months because she moved away, and one patient (the only total nonresponder) continued in treatment for twelve months. Follow-up data were obtained on nine patients after four to twelve months: The eight patients who improved with treatment were all continuing to do well, whereas the one treatment failure remained symptomatic on follow-up.

This study, although uncontrolled, prospectively applied a clearly defined technique and evaluated its efficacy through comprehensive outcome measures. Fairburn (1985) reports continued success with this treatment in over fifty subjects and has begun a controlled study of cognitive behavior therapy versus focused psychotherapy (without behavioral or cognitive features) in bulimia (Fairburn, personal communication).

In the other study assessing individual cognitive behavior therapy, Ordman and Kirschenbaum (1985) treated ten bulimic women for four to twenty-two sessions (average fifteen sessions). Although the time course of treatment was not specified, it appears that sessions were held approximately once a week. The results of treatment for this group were compared to results for ten bulimic women who had been allowed to stay on a waiting list for five months and who had been assessed before and after the waiting period. The active treatment group showed a significant improvement, as compared to waiting-list controls, in frequency of vomiting, number of days on which a binge-purge episode occurred, and measures of eating attitudes, as well as in measures of depression and overall severity of illness. No raw data on the frequency of bingeing or days on which binge-vomit episodes occurred are presented, however; only mean data on frequency of vomiting are mentioned. Vomiting declined from a mean of twelve times per week to a mean of three times per week. No follow-up data are presented.

Several features of this study limit the conclusions that can be

drawn regarding the efficacy of the technique. First, there is a wide variation in the length of treatment given to each patient, from four to twenty-
two sessions; thus, one might question whether all subjects were receiving
a similar form of treatment. Second, no follow-up data are presented.
Outcome data would be particularly useful for evaluating efficacy, given
that the treatment was usually shorter than four months, and one patient
was judged to have responded after only a four-week course of treatment.
Third, the treatment was given by nine graduate students, as opposed to a
single experienced clinician (as in Fairburn's study). It is not clear that
each patient received comparable treatment, although efforts were made to
standardize procedures. Fourth, only mean data on outcome measures
(without range or standard deviation) are presented, and thus it is not
possible to assess whether most subjects had moderate decline in their
symptoms or whether a few subjects got better while the rest failed to
improve. Fifth, the usefulness of waiting-list control groups is questiona-
ble: A waiting list may act as a "reverse placebo," since individuals
on a waiting list may specifically expect not to improve (Prioleau and
others, 1983).

Group Therapy. Group therapy of various types—often combining
elements of various theoretical models of etiology—has become an increasingly common treatment for bulimic patients. It also is the best-studied
psychosocial treatment modality for bulimia.

Group psychotherapy using techniques based on psychodynamic
(Browning, 1985) and feminist (Orbach, 1978) theories have been described,
but no data on the efficacy of these treatments have been reported. Self-
help groups (Larocca and Kolodny, 1983; Larocca, 1984; Rubel, 1984;
Enright and others, 1985), often sponsored by self-help organizations for
eating disorders, have become a welcome addition to the therapeutic
options available for treatment of bulimia. Again, however, there are no
formal studies of the efficacy of this popular and important treatment
modality.

The available reports suffer from so many methodological flaws
that they are virtually uninterpretable. The studies were retrospective, nonblind, and uncontrolled.

Nine additional centers have now presented data on the efficacy of
group therapy for bulimia. Again, most reports are uncontrolled studies.
The following three represent attempts to produce controlled studies.

Lacey (1983, 1985) treated thirty bulimic women with a combination of group and individual sessions, which focused on graduated con-
tracts to modify diet and behavior, as well as on insight-oriented material.
Half the patients were placed directly into the ten-week program. The
other half were kept on a waiting list, without treatment, for ten weeks
and then enrolled in the identical program. During the waiting period, no
significant change in symptoms occurred. (Once again, however, waiting

lists may represent a "reverse placebo.") In both groups, active treatment was associated with a marked decline in frequency of bingeing and vomiting. Regrettably, however, measures of depression and anxiety rose during therapy; one figure suggests that depression scores increased, on the average, by about 50 percent at the conclusion of treatment. Two-year follow-up data were obtained on all thirty patients; twenty sustained a remission of binge-eating, and eight had a reduction of bulimic episodes "to a mean of three times per year."

Johnson and others (1983) and Connors and others (1984) studied the effect of a nine-week group therapy program involving educational, behavioral, and cognitive features in two groups of ten women with bulimia. Treatment was initiated in each group after a two-week assessment period, during which symptoms remained essentially unchanged. In both groups, active treatment was associated with a marked reduction in the frequency of binge-purge episodes, with a mean reduction of 50 percent in the first week and a mean reduction of 70 percent by the end of treatment. Remission of binge-eating was achieved by 15 percent of patients, and 40 percent had decreased their frequency of binge-eating by at least one-half. Scores on measures of eating attitudes and psychological adjustment also improved significantly during treatment.

Pyle and others (1984) and Mitchell and others (1985) have developed a group therapy approach using educational, behavioral, and cognitive techniques in an intensive two-month program. Over 300 patients with bulimia have been treated. Reviewing their immediate posttreatment results with 104 consecutive patients, they found that 47 percent of patients experienced no bulimic behavior from the first session through the entire treatment period, 25 percent had one to three episodes of bulimic behavior, and 11 percent had four or more episodes.

Johnson and others (1983) and Pyle and others (1984) suggest that group therapy may be a promising treatment for bulimia. Both studies are uncontrolled, however, and the data suggest that a substantial placebo effect may have been present. In the Johnson and others (1983) study, there was 50 percent improvement within the first week of subjects' joining the group, and in the Pyle and others (1984) study, 47 percent of subjects stopped bingeing from the moment they entered the group. These observations suggest that expectation for improvement and motivation to improve on the part of the subjects, rather than the therapeutic technique itself, may account for a significant portion of the outcome. Similar reservations must apply to the Lacey (1983, 1985) studies as well. A controlled study—in which half the subjects were assigned to the group therapy to be tested and the other half received, say, conventional psychodynamic therapy—would help to compensate for this placebo effect and would better assess the efficacy of the group therapy techniques themselves.

In addition to several uncontrolled studies that have been reported, two controlled studies of group therapy have been published. Schneider and Agras (1985) developed a cognitive behavioral group treatment, which they initially tested in two pilot groups and then subjected to a controlled study, using a nondirective group therapy approach as the control (Kirkely and others, 1985).

In their initial report, Schneider and Agras (1985) described the treatment of thirteen women (in two groups) with cognitive behavioral therapy in weekly sessions for sixteen weeks. Frequency of vomiting episodes declined from an average of 24 per week to 2.2 per week over the course of treatment, with seven patients achieving a remission of vomiting and an additional four attaining at least a 75 percent reduction in vomiting episodes. Significant improvement in measures of eating attitudes, depression, and assertiveness was also found.

Six-month follow-up data on nine patients revealed that five patients were in remission from vomiting, one was vomiting once per week, three were vomiting between three and five times per week, and two were vomiting fourteen times per week.

After these encouraging preliminary findings, Kirkeley and others (1985) conducted a controlled study of group therapy, in which fourteen women (in two groups) were treated with cognitive behavioral therapy, described above, and fourteen women (also in two groups) were treated with a nondirective group therapy. The only difference between the two treatments was the "presence or absence of specific behavior change recommendations." Both groups were led by two separate pairs of therapists. Each pair of therapists led one cognitive behavioral group and one nondirective group.

Subjects were assigned to one condition or the other, using the minimization-of-differences technique to match the groups on vomiting frequency. Both groups ran for sixteen weeks. What is most important, the investigators assessed the subjects' view of the credibility of treatment: Subjects in both treatment conditions found the treatment highly credible, with essentially no difference between treatment conditions, but there was a trend for more dropouts in the nondirective treatment groups (five cases), as compared to the cognitive behavioral groups (one case).

Both treatments were associated with a decline in the frequency of bingeing and vomiting, but only in the cognitive behavioral groups did the results achieve statistical significance. At the end of the treatment, the subjects treated with cognitive behavior therapy were bingeing and vomiting significantly less than those in nondirective treatment. On measures of depression, anxiety, and eating attitudes, subjects in both treatments improved significantly, and no significant differences between treatment conditions were found. Thus, immediate posttreatment evaluation showed a significant superiority of cognitive behavior treatment on only one index—the frequency of bingeing and vomiting—but showed no differences between the groups on other indices.

Because of the small differences observed between treatments, it is difficult to amass much support for the cognitive behavioral approach. It could be argued that cognitive behavior therapy has an advantage over nondirective treatment in short-term effects and, further, that it may lead to fewer dropouts from treatment. A difference in short-term results was present on only a single outcome measure, however, and even this difference had disappeared after three months.

Unfortunately, like most studies of psychosocial treatments, this one could be conducted only as a single-blind study; the subjects did not know which treatment was the control, but the investigators did. Furthermore, in this study, both treatments were run by the same therapists. Although this design ensures that intertherapist variation does not account for the difference observed between treatment groups, the possibility of observer bias is introduced. Specifically, the therapists, who may have had an interest in finding cognitive behavioral treatment more effective than nondirective treatment, somehow may have influenced the relative performance of the two groups. Given that experimenter bias has been shown to influence (unconsciously) the assessment of character (Harvey, 1938), the perception of success or failure of individuals on the basis of facial photographs (Rosenthal and others, 1963), and even the performance of maze-running rats (Rosenthal and Fode, 1963), this potential source of bias must be considered carefully, especially in light of the observation that the two treatment groups converged to similar outcomes three months after treatment.

Another controlled study of group therapy was performed by Freeman and others (1985), in which patients were randomly assigned to group therapy, individual behavior therapy, or individual cognitive therapy. This study found no significant difference on outcome measures between the three treatments, with the exception that group therapy—unlike behavioral and cognitive therapy—was not associated with significant reductions in self-ratings of depression and anxiety (although levels of depression, as assessed on a clinician-rated instrument, did decrease significantly among those receiving group therapy). In contrast to the Kirkely and others (1985) study, no attempt was made to construct a nonspecific "placebo" treatment. The group therapy employed, however, used less specific techniques than the individual behavioral and cognitive treatments did.

These last two studies—one finding no significant differences among three active treatments, and the other finding essentially no differences between an active treatment and a nonspecific "placebo" treatment—again raise the question of whether successful outcome in psychotherapy of bulimia is due to specific factors or simply to such nonspecific factors as sympathetic human contact.

Many centers have developed eating-disorders clinics that have treated patients with eclectic programs combining elements of individual or group psychotherapy and sometimes pharmacotherapy. A variety of other psychosocial treatments for bulimia have been reported, including inpatient treatment (Larocca, 1984; Lacey, 1985) and residential outpatient treatment (Wooley and Wooley, 1985), but no studies have appeared that have assessed response to these modalities.

Pharmacological Treatment

Thymoleptics. More than twenty-five reports, including five placebo-controlled double-blind studies, have assessed the efficacy of thymoleptic medications—that is, medications used to treat major affective disorder—in the treatment of bulimia.

Early Studies. Following three case reports of successful treatment of bulimia with amitriptyline (Moore, 1977) or phenelzine (Rich, 1978; Shader and Greenblatt, 1982), two series of cases of bulimic patients treated with antidepresssants were published in 1982. Pope and Hudson (1982) described eight patients with bulimia, who were treated primarily with imipramine or desipramine. With medication, six experienced at least 50 percent decrease in frequency of bingeing. Three of these had greater than 90 percent decrease in bingeing. The patients maintained their improvement on medication over follow-up periods of two to seven months.

Walsh and others (1982), using monoamine oxidase inhibitors (MAOIs) (phenelzine or tranylcypromine) in six bulimic patients, also described encouraging results: Four achieved remission of bingeing, and two reduced frequency of bingeing to once or twice per month. On follow-up, one patient relapsed after one month. The total follow-up periods for the other patients is not specified.

In early 1983, there followed several other anecdotal reports of successful treatment of bulimia with tricyclic antidepressants (Mendels, 1983; Roy-Byrne and others, 1983) and MAOIs (Jonas and others, 1983).

Placebo-Controlled Studies with Antidepressants. These promising uncontrolled findings prompted a series of placebo-controlled double-blind studies with various antidepressants in bulimia. Five such studies have appeared to date.

In the first, Sabine and others (1983) assessed the antidepressant mianserin versus placebo in fifty patients with Bulimia Nervosa. Twenty patients were randomized to mianserin, 60 mg per day, and thirty received placebo. There were fourteen dropouts during the eight weeks of the study—six in the mianserin group and eight in the placebo group. During the study, both the mianserin group and the placebo group improved significantly on many measures, including ratings of depression and anxiety, as well as on a "bulimia rating scale" of the authors' design. On one measure of eating attitudes, the placebo group improved significantly, whereas the mianserin group did not. The number of days per week during which the subjects reported binge-eating or vomiting, however, did not change in either group.

Several aspects of the study deserve consideration. To begin with, the study suggests that many bulimic patients improve with brief clinic visits plus placebo alone. These observations—like those of Johnson and others (1983) and Pyle and others (1984)—underline the need to allow for the placebo effect in evaluating uncontrolled reports of any form of treatment for bulimia. Next, the Sabine and others (1983) study appears to suggest that mianserin is ineffective for bulimia. For several reasons, however, this interpretation may be incorrect. First, the dose of mianserin used (60 mg per day) may have been too low. One study (McGrath and others, 1981) reported that daily doses of up to 150 mg were required to produce an antidepressant effect. Second, most subjects were engaging in purging behavior, which might have interfered with adequate absorption of the drug, leading to subtherapeutic antidepressant plasma levels in many subjects. Third, in this study, mianserin was virtually indistinguishable from placebo on any measure of depression. Although this observation admits to multiple interpretations, at least it is consistent with the possibility that inadequate levels of mianserin were achieved in the subjects. Thus, it seems premature to judge the efficacy of mianserin in the treatment of bulimia on the basis of this one study.

In a second placebo-controlled double-blind study, Pope and others (1983) administered imipramine versus placebo to twenty-two women with bulimia. Half the subjects were randomized to imipramine 200 mg per day and half to placebo. There were three dropouts (two on imipramine, one on placebo). At the end of the six-week study period, the frequency of bingeing had declined by about 70 percent in the imipramine groups but was virtually unchanged in the placebo group. In terms of individual response among those treated with imipramine, no subject achieved remission from binge-eating, but four experienced greater than 75 percent reduction in frequency of bingeing, another four had greater than 50 percent reduction in frequency of bingeing, and one remained unimproved. Hamilton Rating Scale for Depression (HRSD) scores declined nearly 50 percent in the imipramine group but only 1 percent in the placebo group. Significant differences were also found on several subjective measures of eating behavior and attitudes, as well as on subjective global improvement. Improvement in depression and decreases in frequency of bingeing were significantly correlated.

Two-year follow-up data on these subjects have been presented in a subsequent report (Pope and others, in press). Placebo subjects were offered treatment with imipramine or other antidepressants at the end of the six-week study period. Imipramine-treated subjects were continued on imipramine or were switched to other antidepressants if there were suboptimal responses or problems with side-effects. Of the twenty subjects who received antidepressant treatment during and/or after the double-blind phase of the study, eleven were followed for more than two years, four were followed between one and two years, and five were lost to follow-up in less than one year. At the end of the last follow-up, ten of the subjects had achieved remission of bingeing, an additional three had experienced at least 75 percent reduction in frequency of bingeing, six others had experienced at least 50 percent reduction in frequency of bingeing, and one was unimproved. Of the ten remitted subjects, three had been able to discontinue medication at some time during the follow-up period, without relapse. The other seven patients remained on various antidepressants. These data suggest that the beneficial effect of antidepressants is maintained over the long term. The authors, however, noted that in many subjects long-term treatment with antidepressants was quite complicated, often requiring considerable experimentation with different medications.

In a third placebo-controlled study, Walsh and others (1984) administered the MAOI phenelzine, in doses of up to 90 mg per day, versus placebo to twenty-five bulimia patients. There were five dropouts (two in the placebo group and three in the phenelzine group) and twenty completers. Phenelzine proved significantly superior to placebo on frequency of bingeing and on measures of eating attitudes. HRSD scores were reduced, but not significantly so, in the phenelzine group.

When HRSD items that were possibly related to phenelzine side-effects (for example, insomnia) were excluded, however, this difference became significant. In terms of individual response, five of the nine phenelzine patients achieved remission of bingeing episodes, and three others experienced at least 50 percent reduction in frequency of bingeing. The authors noted that troublesome side-effects, particularly hypotension, were experienced by many subjects treated with phenelzine.

In a fourth study of twenty-two bulimic patients, Hughes and others (in press) assigned ten to desipramine 200 mg per day and twelve to placebo, for six weeks. Patients with major depression were excluded—a criterion not applied to previous studies. On all outcome measures, including frequency of bingeing as well as measures of depression and eating attitudes, desipramine was significantly superior to placebo. Frequency of bingeing decreased by an average of 91 percent in the desipramine group, as compared to a 19 percent increase in the placebo group. All the placebo subjects received open trial of desipramine at the conclusion of the blind phase of the study. At the end of ten weeks, fifteen (68 percent) of the total group of twenty-two subjects had attained remission of bingeing, and an additional four subjects had shown at least 75 percent reduction in frequency of binge-eating.

A further feature of this study deserves comment. Unlike previous groups, Hughes and others measured plasma levels of antidepressants. Fourteen (70 percent) of twenty subjects tested were found to be outside the therapeutic range for desipramine (125–275 mg/ml at the Mayo Clinic Laboratories). Ten were below the lower limit of this range. Four of these ten were already in remission from bingeing, and so their dosages were not adjusted. In the remaining six, dosages were adjusted upward to achieve therapeutic plasma levels, and four of these subjects—one requiring 350 mg per day of desipramine—then achieved remission of symptoms. In the four subjects whose desipramine levels appeared too high, dosage was reduced, with improvement in side-effects and no deterioration of clinical response.

These findings emphasize the importance of achieving adequate levels of antidepressant medication in the treatment of bulimia, and they support the possibility that the negative findings of Sabine and others (1983) with mianserin and the modest (although positive) findings of Pope and others (1983) with imipramine might have been improved had these investigators been able to ensure adequate dosage in all their subjects.

Adequate dosage again appears to be a factor in a fifth placebo-controlled double-blind study of 32 bulimic patients, in which Mitchell and Groat (1984) randomized sixteen patients to amitriptyline 150 mg and sixteen to placebo. Six subjects dropped out of the study (five on amitriptyline and one on placebo) and were replaced. Amitriptyline was not significantly superior to placebo on the Zung rating scale (Zung, 1965) for depression but was significantly superior to placebo on the HRSD. It is interesting that both the amitriptyline and the placebo groups improved on all measures of eating behavior.

Antidepressant plasma levels were measured in eight of the sixteen subjects on active drug. Of these, one had a plasma level of zero (indicating probable noncompliance) and three others had combined amitriptyline and nortriptyline levels of less than 75 mg/ml—a value below the therapeutic range suggested by most studies of amitriptyline plasma levels (Braithwaite and others, 1972; Zeigler and others, 1977). This observation not only implies that as many as 50 percent of the subjects in this study may have received inadequate doses of amitriptyline; perhaps it also explains why the study yielded weaker results than the other two studies of tricyclic antidepressants that we have discussed here.

In summary, five placebo-controlled double-blind studies have tested antidepressant medications for bulimia. Three have produced clearly positive findings (Pope and others, 1983; Walsh and others, 1984; Hughes and others, in press), one a weakly positive finding (Mitchell and Groat, 1984), and one a negative finding (Sabine and others, 1983). It appears that many subjects in the latter two studies, however, may have had inadequate plasma levels of medications.

Conclusion

1. Of the available treatment modalities for bulimia reported in the literature, antidepressant medications are the best established in methodo-

logically sound studies, including four positive placebo-controlled studies. Bulimic patients are candidates for antidepressant treatment, whether or not they have concomitant major depression or a family history of major affective disorder.

2. The best-studied psychosocial treatments are individual cognitive behavioral therapy and group therapy, the latter generally with cognitive, behavioral, and educational features. The only two controlled studies of these modalities—involving (a) behavior therapy versus cognitive therapy versus group therapy and (b) cognitive behavioral group therapy versus nondirective group therapy—failed to show any significant differences in outcome among the various treatments under study. Thus, it is not clear from these studies whether the beneficial results were attributable to specific techniques or to the nonspecific effects of sympathetic human contact. The remaining studies are uncontrolled, making them difficult to evaluate, given the possibility of a placebo effect and the fact that bulimia may remit spontaneously. Thus, although both individual and group therapies may indeed be effective, it is not possible to recommend one form of psychosocial treatment over another. Further controlled studies of psychosocial treatments should command high priority for subsequent research in the treatment of bulimia.

3. Long-term efficacy has not been well established for any treatment modality, although unsystematic studies suggest that individual cognitive behavioral treatment, group therapy, and antidepressant treatment may all be associated with good long-term results.

4. No study employing a combination of psychosocial and pharmacological treatments has been performed. Such a study, using either individual or group cognitive behavioral techniques and either a tricyclic antidepressant or an MAOI, would be particularly welcome.

References

Braithwaite, R. A., Goulding, R., Theano, G., Bailey, J., and Coppen, A. "Plasma Concentration of Amitriptyline and Clinical Response." *Lancet*, 1972, *1*, 1297–1300.

Browning, W. N. "Long-Term Dynamic Group Therapy with Bulimic Patients: A Clinical Discussion." In S. W. Emmett (ed.), *Theory and Treatment of Anorexia Nervosa and Bulimia*. New York: Brunner/Mazel, 1985.

Connors, M. E., Johnson, C. L., and Stuckey, M. K. "Treatment of Bulimia with Brief Psychoeducational Group Therapy." *American Journal of Psychiatry*, 1984, *141*, 1512–1516.

Enright, A. B., Butterfield, P., and Berkowitz, B. "Self-Help and Support Groups in the Management of Eating Disorders." In D. M. Garner and P. E. Garfinkel (eds.), *Handbook of Psychotherapy for Anorexia Nervosa and Bulimia*. New York: Guilford Press, 1985.

Fairburn, C. G. "A Cognitive Behavioral Approach to the Treatment of Bulimia." *Psychological Medicine*, 1981, *11*, 707–711.

Fairburn, C. G. "Cognitive-Behavioral Treatment for Bulimia." In D. M. Garner and P. E. Garfinkel (eds.), *Handbook of Psychotherapy for Anorexia Nervosa and Bulimia*. New York: Guilford Press, 1985.

Freeman, C., Sinclair, F., Turnbull, J., and Annandale, A. "Psychotherapy for Bulimia: A Controlled Study." *Journal of Psychiatric Research*, 1985, *19*, 473–478.

Grinc, G. A. "A Cognitive-Behavioral Model for the Treatment of Chronic Vomiting." *Journal of Behavioral Medicine*, 1982, *1*, 135–141.

Harvey, S. M. "A Preliminary Investigation of the Interview." *British Journal of Psychiatry*, 1938, *28*, 263–287.

Hughes, P. L., Wells, L. A., Cunningham, C. J., and Ilstrup, D. M. "Treating Bulimia with Desipramine: A Placebo-Controlled Double-Blind Study." *Archives of General Psychiatry*, in press.

Johnson, C. L., Connors, M., and Stuckey, M. "Short-Term Group Treatment of Bulimia: A Preliminary Report." *International Journal of Eating Disorders*, 1983, *2*, 199–208.

Jonas, J. M., Hudson, J. I., and Pope, H. G., Jr. "Eating Disorders and Antidepressants" (letter). *Journal of Clinical Psychopharmacology*, 1983, *3*, 59–60.

Kenny, F. T., and Solyom, L. "The Treatment of Compulsive Vomiting Through Faradic Disruption of Mental Images." *Canadian Medical Association Journal*, 1971, *105*, 1072–1073.

Kirkely, B. G., Schneider, J. A., Agras, W. S., and Bachman, J. A. "Comparison of Two Group Treatments for Bulimia." *Journal of Consulting and Clinical Psychology*, 1985, *53*, 43–58.

Lacey, J. H. "Bulimia Nervosa, Binge Eating, and Psychogenic Vomiting: A Controlled Treatment Study and Long-Term Outcome." *British Medical Journal*, 1983, *286*, 1609–1613.

Lacey, J. H. "Time-Limited Individual and Group Treatment for Bulimia." In D. M. Garner and P. E. Garfinkel (eds.), *Handbook of Psychotherapy for Anorexia Nervosa and Bulimia*. New York: Guilford Press, 1985.

Larocca, F.E.F. "An Inpatient Model for the Treatment of Eating Disorders." *Psychiatric Clinics of North America*, 1984, 7 (2), 287–298.

Larocca, F.E.F., and Kolodny, N. J. *Anorexia and Bulimia. Facilitator's Manual—A Primer: The BASH Approach*. St. Louis: Midwest Medical Publications, 1983.

Leitenberg, H., Gross, J., Peterson, J., and Rosen, J. C. "Analysis of an Anxiety Model and the Process of Change During Exposure Plus Response Prevention Treatment of Bulimia Nervosa." *Behavior Therapy*, 1984, *15*, 3–20.

Linden, W. "Multi-Component Behavior Therapy in a Case of Compulsive Binge-Eating Followed by Vomiting." *Journal of Behavior Therapy and Experimental Psychiatry*, 1980, *11*, 212–215.

Long, C. G., and Cordle, C. J. "Psychological Treatment of Binge Eating and Self-Induced Vomiting." *British Journal of Medical Psychology*, 1982, *55*, 139–145.

McGrath, P. J., Quitkin, F. M., Stewart, J. W., Liebowitz, M., Fyer, A., and Davies, S. "An Open Clinical Trial of Mianserin." *American Journal of Psychiatry*, 1981, *138*, 530–532.

Mendels, J. "Eating Disorders and Antidepressants" (letter). *Journal of Clinical Psychopharmacology*, 1983, *3*, 59.

Mitchell, J. E., and Groat, R. "A Placebo-Controlled, Double-Blind Trial of Amitriptyline in Bulimia." *Journal of Clinical Psychopharmacology*, 1984, *4*, 186–193.

Mitchell, J. E., Hatsukami, D., Goff, G., Pyle, R. L., Eckert, E. D., and Davis, L. E. "Intensive Outpatient Group Treatment for Bulimia." In D. M. Garner and P. E. Garfinkel (eds.), *Handbook of Psychotherapy for Anorexia Nervosa and Bulimia*. New York: Guilford Press, 1985.

Mizes, J. S., and Lohr, S. M. "The Treatment of Bulimia (Binge-Eating and Self-Induced Vomiting)." *International Journal of Eating Disorders*, 1983, *2*, 59–65.

Monti, P. M., McCrady, B. S., and Barlow, D. H. "Effect of Positive Reinforcement, Informational Feedback, and Contingency Contracting on a Bulimia Anorexic Female." *Behavior Therapy*, 1977, *8*, 258–263.

Moore, D. C. "Amitriptyline Therapy for Anorexia Nervosa." *American Journal of Psychiatry*, 1977, *134*, 1303–1304.

Orbach, S. *Fat Is a Feminist Issue*. London: Paddington Press, 1978.

Ordman, A. M., and Kirschenbaum, D. S. "Cognitive-Behavioral Therapy for Bulimia: An Initial Outcome Study." *Journal of Consulting and Clinical Psychology*, 1985, *53*, 305–311.

Pope, H. G., Jr., and Hudson, J. I. "Treatment of Bulimia with Antidepressants." *Psychopharmacology*, 1982, *78*, 167–179.

Pope, H. G., Jr., Hudson, J. I., Jonas, J. M., and Yurgelun-Todd, D. "Bulimia Treated with Imipramine: A Placebo-Controlled, Double-Blind Study." *American Journal of Psychiatry*, 1983, *140* (5), 554–558.

Pope, H. G., Jr., Hudson, J. I., Jonas, J. M., and Yurgelun-Todd, D. "Antidepressant Treatment of Bulimia: A Two-Year Follow-Up Study." *Journal of Clinical Psychopharmacology*, in press.

Prioleau, L., Murdock, M., and Brody, N. "An Analysis of Psychotherapy Versus Placebo Studies." *The Behavioral and Brain Sciences*, 1983, *6*, 275–310.

Pyle, R. L., Eckert, E. D., Hatsukami, D. K., and Goff, G. "The Interruption of Bulimic Behaviors." *Psychiatric Clinics of North America*, 1984, *7*, 275–286.

Rich, C. L. "Self-Induced Vomiting: Psychiatric Considerations." *Journal of the American Medical Association*, 1978, *239*, 2688–2689.

Rosen, J. C., and Leitenberg, H. "Bulimia Nervosa: Treatment with Exposure and Response Prevention." *Behavior Therapy*, 1982, *13*, 117–124.

Rosenthal, R., and Fode, K. L. "The Effect of Experimenter Bias on the Performance of the Albino Rat." *Behavioral Science*, 1963, *8*, 183–189.

Rosenthal, R., Persinger, G. W., Kline, V. L., and Mulry, R. C. "The Role of the Research Assistant in the Mediation of Experimenter Bias." *Journal of Personality*, 1963, *31*, 313–335.

Roy-Byrne, P., Gwirtsman, H., Edelstein, C. K., Yager, J., and Gerner, R. H. "Eating Disorders and Antidepressants" (letter). *Journal of Clinical Psychopharmacology*, 1983, *3*, 60–61.

Rubel, J. A. "The Function of Self-Help Groups in Recovery from Anorexia Nervosa." *Psychiatric Clinics of North America*, 1984, *7*, 381–394.

Sabine, E. J., Yonace, A., Farrington, A. J., Barratt, K. H., and Wakeling, A. "Bulimia Nervosa: A Placebo-Controlled Double-Blind Therapeutic Trial of Mianserin." *British Journal of Clinical Pharmacology*, 1983, *15*, 1955–2025.

Schneider, J. A., and Agras, W. S. "A Cognitive Behavioral Group Treatment of Bulimia." *British Journal of Psychiatry*, 1985, *146*, 66–69.

Schwartz, R. C. "Bulimia and Family Therapy: A Case Study." *International Journal of Eating Disorders*, 1982, *2*, 75–82.

Schwartz, R. C., Barrett, M. J., and Saba, G. "Family Therapy for Bulimia." In D. M. Garner and P. E. Garfinkel (eds.), *Handbook of Psychotherapy for Anorexia Nervosa and Bulimia*. New York: Guilford Press, 1985.

Shader, R. I., and Greenblatt, D. J. "The Psychiatrist as Mind Sweeper." *Journal of Clinical Psychopharmacology*, 1982, *2*, 233–234.

Walsh, B. T., Stewart, J. W., Roose, S. P., Gladis, M., and Glassman, A. H. "Treatment of Bulimia with Phenelzine: A Double-Blind, Placebo-Controlled Study." *Archives of General Psychiatry*, 1984, *41*, 1105–1110.

Walsh, B. T., Stewart, J. W., Wright, L., Harrison, W., Roose, S. P., and Glassman, A. H. "Treatment of Bulimia with Monoamine Oxidase Inhibitors." *American Journal of Psychiatry*, 1982, *139* (12), 1629-1630.

Welch, G. J. "The Treatment of Compulsive Vomiting and Obsessive Thoughts Through Graduated Response Delay, Response Prevention and Cognitive Correction." *Journal of Behavior Therapy and Experimental Psychiatry*, 1979, *10*, 77-82.

Wooley, S. C., and Wooley, O. W. "Intensive Outpatient and Residential Treatment for Bulimia." In D. M. Garner and P. E. Garfinkel (eds.), *Handbook of Psychotherapy for Anorexia Nervosa and Bulimia*. New York: Guilford Press, 1985.

Zeigler, V. E., Clayton, P. J., and Biggs, J. T. "A Comparison Study of Amitriptyline and Nortriptyline with Plasma Levels." *Archives of General Psychiatry*, 1977, *34*, 607-612.

Zung, W.W.K. "A Self-Rating Depression Scale." *Archives of General Psychiatry*, 1965, *12*, 63-70.

James I. Hudson is assistant professor of psychiatry at Harvard Medical School in Boston, Massachusetts, and associate chief, Epidemiology Laboratory, The Mailman Research Center at McLean Hospital in Belmont, Massachusetts.

Harrison G. Pope, Jr., is associate professor of psychiatry at Harvard Medical School in Boston, Massachusetts, and chief, Epidemiology Laboratory, The Mailman Research Center at McLean Hospital in Belmont, Massachusetts.

Selections from a patient's writings to her therapist highlight the stages of recovery when nasogastric tube feeding was used in the treatment of a restrictive anorectic.

Tube Feeding: Is It Ever Necessary?

Félix E. F. Larocca, Sherry A. Goodner

Dietary information still remains an essential part of any eating-disorders treatment program. Although patients with eating disorders appear to have above-average information about nutrition, some professionals believe that this information is inadequate with regard to basic nutritional concepts. Knowledge about calories does not necessarily mean understanding of nutrition. Some treatment programs offer the services of dietitians to help patients gain information and increase awareness of their nutritional needs and the effects of malnutrition on their bodies. Even with nutritional information and services available through on-unit dietary support, however, a need remains occasionally for a more invasive form of nutritional treatment.

The authors of this chapter, who have treated scores of anorectics and bulimics as inpatients, outpatients, and intermediate-care patients, will grapple with the issue of whether some forms of invasive treatment, such as nasogastric tube feeding (NGTF), are justifiable. Also to be discussed is whether this treatment approach works and, if so, how.

Most clinicians who treat eating disorders consider nutritional rehabilitation essential in overall care (Bruch, 1973). Refeeding may be carried out in a variety of ways. To some doctors, this is an impersonal approach. To other professionals, the approach is mechanical, casual, and even incidental. In some programs, it is an idea that is plainly rejected.

F.E.F. Larocca (ed.). *Eating Disorders.*
New Directions for Mental Health Services, no. 31. San Francisco: Jossey-Bass, Fall 1986.

For some, weight is not essential, while for others it is a most essential feature. In some cases, weight is negotiated, established, and adhered to as part of an inviolable contract. In others, it is a negotiable, flexible, and important issue subject to review and revision during treatment.

The purpose of this chapter is to outline a tube-feeding method, based on theoretical constructs and empirical observations, that takes into account all aspects of the individual's personality and uniqueness.

The restrictive nutritional intake of an anorectic or a low-weight bulimic may produce a state of semistarvation. The significance of these losses as a result of restrictive intake may lead to ketoacidosis. If ketonemia becomes severe, insulin secretion will be stimulated and a feedback control will ensue, since insulin inhibits ketogenesis. This feedback mechanism aids the body in avoiding pathological ketoacidosis (Krause and Mahan, 1984; Green and Greene, 1984).

Consequently, efforts at renourishing the patient are indeed justifiable and at times necessary for overall treatment. The medical complications that may arise if treatment does not initially address nutritional rehabilitation are primarily related to the effects of starvation on the body. Herzog and Copeland (1985) in their review of medical progress in treating eating disorders, refer to as high as a 9 percent mortality rate associated with Anorexia Nervosa (excluding suicide).

Vandereycken and Meermann (1984) review the positions that several authors have taken, including Andersen (1984), who considers nasogastric feeding to be a failure: "It is all too often used prematurely and punitively." Vandereycken and Meermann state:

> It seems to us, however, that tube feeding, just like ECT, has become an emotionally controversial symbol of so-called repressive psychiatry. Though we are not defending either method, we feel that very often the possibly deleterious effect does not primarily depend on the method itself, but on its users (i.e., the therapeutic context). That's why we would prefer, in certain circumstances, tube feeding to . . . more subtle manipulation [Vandereycken and Meermann, 1984, p. 92].

Andersen and others (1985) emphasize two specific points concerning weight gain. Experience indicates that even more important than weight gain is to develop helpful attitudes concerning issues such as nutrition, role modeling, and working out the patient's fear of fatness in psychotherapy. Weight is viewed as a means to an end and not an end in itself. Many confusing symptoms are produced by starvation, thus rendering psychotherapy ineffective. Thus, weight gain by itself is only the beginning of the process of healing (Andersen and others, 1985).

Halmi (1982) purports the use of behavior therapy for the treatment of Anorexia Nervosa and refers to the use of tube feeding as a negative reinforcer. She states, "Others have included powerful negative reinforcements, such as bedrest, isolation, and tube feeding. The most effective behavior therapy programs are individualized, that is, a behavior therapy program is set up only after a behavioral analysis of the patient is completed."

Tube Feeding à la BASH

Our approach requires the patient to be made aware that weight gains are accomplished with the assistance of a dietitian and nutritional supplements. The patient needs to know that adequate monitoring of energy expenditure is now forthcoming, and that bulimic behaviors have ravaged his or her weight, resulting in an over 25 percent body-weight loss, or a significant loss from the expected standard weight for an individual, according to the norm. Our approach is a negotiated, nonviolent, nonpunitive, delicate effort in which (1) the patient is asked to cooperate in overcoming the fear of gaining weight, (2) trust is expressed by the patient's submitting to a procedure in which faith in the individual practitioner is important, as in the case of general anesthesia, and (3) the goal is not to "pump" pounds into the patient, but rather to allow the patient to become acquainted with himself or herself at a normal or close-to-normal weight.

The Negotiation

After admission to the hospital, patients are kept informed of weight fluctuations, but not of the exact figures (Larocca, 1984). Distortions (such as when patients feel they are gaining excessive amounts of weight) are corrected via individual and group psychotherapeutic contacts. Patients become aware that even though they feel their clothing is now bursting at the seams, the fact is that after two weeks of hospitalization, they are losing and have lost gradually. They are then introduced to dietary supplements. The dietitian helps patients choose the right kinds of food. Now the issue for patients becomes one of control.

On occasion, a patient refuses the supplements (which should not be forced), and no punitive measures of any kind are taken. The staff does, however, make frequent notations concerning the patient's feelings, as well as his or her refusal of supplements. Statements reflecting the patient's growing fear of obesity are also noted but not dealt with in a punitive manner. Because the health factors of malnutrition are hazardous, however, tube feeding is indicated. Eventually, after meeting with patient and family for a discussion of the tube-feeding process, nasogastric tube feeding (NGTF) begins. The evaluation is carried out in a manner that is standardized in our unit by the nutritional support team.

For the NGTF process, the patient has to be on absolute bed rest. She wears only hospital scrubs and has no access to the phone, visitors, or regular physical activities. The rate of the feeding starts at 50, 75, or 100 cc/hr progressively, as indicated by the nutritional support team. The patient is also made aware of the rate, as the feeding pump displays the type of feeding formula used and the rate at which it is being administered. The patient is aware from these visual cues of the possibility that she is gaining weight during the tube-feeding process.

Privileges are allowed on a daily basis, according to the anticipated effect of the increased activity level during the weight-gain process. Examples of such privileges are a daily shower, watching TV in the evening with peers, and socializing with other patients. Privileges are evaluated daily to assess their effect on weight gain, as well as on the patient's attitude.

We are aware of some resistance that may be expressed by the patient's disconnecting the pump or exercising during the night, or using the formula surreptitiously for such things as watering the plants. This is neither condemned nor condoned, however. The patient is simply made aware that the process is a frightening one, and that we are there to help her overcome anxiety and fear. While the nursing staff makes no effort to spend extra time with the patient (making her "special" among all the other patients), there is concern among the staff for increased awareness of the patient's needs and of how she may choose to express them. Nurses have a unique opportunity for such assessment while attending to the tube-feeding process itself. For example, during irrigation of the nasogastric tube, the nurse can assess the patient for complaints of epigastric distress, as well as for concerns over the increased food intake. Such statements as "But how can you expect me to eat when I have this stuff going in my stomach all day long?" inform the nurse that the patient continues to need correct dietary information. A sensitive but firm and consistent approach by all staff members enhances trust and allows the patient to begin working through the feelings she fears most.

The patient is also involved in all therapeutic activities. On such occasions (for example, BASH meetings that are open to the public), she may have an opportunity to meet her family, even though she is not allowed to see them routinely in the hospital. As the NGTF progresses and the patient becomes aware of certain physiological changes taking place (such as secondary sexual characteristics that develop in the immature child), the negotiation of a steady, stable weight is then contracted. Since the patient eats during the time she is on NGTF, she is aware that the more food she consumes, the sooner the tubes will be discontinued.

In one case, extensive notes were written by a patient who experienced the tube-feeding process. These notes showed the three phases a patient moves through when refeeding is utilized during recovery. All these phases are not traveled through while a patient is on NGTF. We believe, however, that the refeeding process allows the patient mobility into all three phases. The issue of control is both complex and paralyzing for a patient with an eating disorder. Utilizing NGTF during the refeeding process can often allow the patient to move beyond the issue of control.

The three phases are (1) initiation and panic, (2) actual surrender, and (3) the period of hope. Phase 1 reveals the patient as volatile in expressing emotions. The patient relentlessly defends the pursuit of thinness, both verbally and physically. During this phase one may find a patient exercising in bed or feeding her supplement to her plant.

Phase 2 is composed of three stages: struggle, sorting, and redefinition. The surrender begins with the patient resisting the acceptance of change. There is struggle in accepting physical changes (weight gain) during nutritional rehabilitation, as well as in accepting the emotions and feelings that arise during this time. In addition, there is a struggle in accepting the way others will perceive her after this change has occurred. (Some fear rejection after they have become "fattened up.") The next step in surrender is sorting through emotions and physical changes, and assigning values to these changes. There is not always linear progression between these two steps. Rather, these are dynamic forces that create ambivalence in the patient's verbal and physical behavior. There is eventual progress to the third stage of phase 2. This is the redefinition of values concerning weight, body image, and self-worth. The patient becomes aware of a decision to relinquish the old values assigned to these aspects of the struggle and to pursue the redefinition of those values. Even at this step, however, the patient may continue to sort through the struggles with body changes, acceptance and awareness of her emotions, and concern over acceptance by significant others. The time spent in sorting will be less than during the initial struggle, however.

Phase 3, the period of hope, is an evolving stage for the patient and demands time free from constraints. During this period, the patient may reflect on the struggle to surrender and may even question the wisdom of deciding to moving forward through that struggle, but she nevertheless continues in that direction. Emotions continue to be sorted through and redefined as the forward progression continues. The patient often may define hope as elusive or intangible, but she continues to recognize its presence and its effect on recovery.

Case Study

The following case, based on the notes of a patient whose identity has been disguised, illustrates the NGTF process.

The patient was fifteen years old and came to BASH from out of state. She was referred to us after failing to respond twice to treatment at a hometown hospital. Her family had taken the trip to St. Louis in a last-

92

ditch effort to save her life. A number of practitioners had tried to assist the family in promoting her care, but this assistance was almost totally ineffective. One of the most disappointing efforts came from a self-appointed dietitian, who had opened an office advertising that she was a specialist in the treatment of anorexia and bulimia. The counseling was that the patient should stick to the four basic food groups and that the family should leave the patient alone. This was a catastrophic and frustrating experience, leading the family to go to a practitioner who simply put the patient on antidepressants and told the parents to weigh her daily and see that she gained the weight back. Nothing helped, and her parents then made the trip to see us.

The patient at first appeared reluctant to be involved. She seemed forlorn about her family's decision and their being so far away. She was particularly unimpressed by the need to gain some weight. She was happy, however, when all medications were discontinued. Gradually, during the first two weeks of her hospital stay, her weight dropped. Her weight on admission, 34 kg, dropped to 32.7 kg over fifteen days in the hospital. She was then acquainted with the possibility of tube feedings. Her parents agreed that lifesaving measures had to begin.

The following are excerpts from the patient's writings to her therapist. The first excerpt offers a view of the patient early in the treatment process, soon after admission and just prior to the initiation of NGTF:

> I feel like I'm up against a brick wall. When someone says, "How are your meals coming?" I automatically say, "I'm scared to death of food and don't want to eat." Or if they say, "You're skinny," I'll say, "No, I'm not. I'm fat." Things like that. It feels mechanical, like I have to say it. It's like if I don't, I don't know what would happen. Today a couple of girls were telling me they weighed themselves, and one weighed as much as I did. I have to gain weight, and she doesn't. It's not fair. I can write down, "I don't want to try, I don't want to get better or give this up." It's what I've been saying, but I can honestly say I don't feel it in my heart. I'm afraid to admit I have a problem, to get better, to try, because my control that I've had for so long will be fading. I want to trust you. I'm having a hard time trusting myself. I'm scared to admit it may be because of the fact that it's going to take so long, and I still have strong feelings of: What else is there? The fear of eating three square meals a day, liking it, and not being able to stop; I'm afraid I'll keep gaining.

Phase 1. She was unable to gain weight by relying on her own efforts, and so the decision was made to initiate NGTF. The following excerpt from her letters illustrates phase 1, initiation and panic:

My attitude was "Oh, no way, not me, I'm not letting them stick a tube down me." When it happened, I also took it as a punishment. I was frantic. It was strange, though; that whole day I was in good spirits all day. It was almost like I didn't know how to react. They told me three meals and four Ensures and the tube. I was overwhelmed, but I just said, "That's going to be so hard, I can't eat that much." They said, "You can do it." I didn't say anything. The next day, I was in pretty good spirits again, only a little more down. Next day a little more down. Then today I got even more restricted. I have nothing left. I should be so angry, and I think I am, but it's buried. I think my anger is mainly at myself, though. I'm so sick of all this! I feel like a freak, and a weakling. My feelings of wanting to trust, to try, are there, but they're getting overruled. The strength is so tremendous. What am I clinging to? It's so hard for me to understand why I just won't let go. The control is gone, maybe I'm trying to get it back, but I don't want to stay here for the rest of my life. Trust! I know it's supposed to come with time, but meanwhile, I lie here with nothing. I found myself today arguing with people that this is just going to get me fat, that I don't need it. Deep down, I'm yelling, "Stop!"

Phase 2. After several days on tube feedings, phase, 2, the struggle to surrender, became apparent:

I've been dwelling on my weight gain for the last couple of days. It's been getting me down. I accidentally saw my weight Friday morning: 94 pounds. It really got me down. He better not make me 100 pounds. I'll go home and lose till 95 pounds if he does. I've been thinking about my clothes, how people at home are going to accept it, and stuff like that. I can't see my bones anymore. My gut is huge! Everyone keeps telling me how healthy I look. My face is puffier, and in some way it looks better. But I keep thinking *fat* instead of *healthy*. I won't let go. I wonder if worrying about "fat" is a cover-up for some other feeling. But my pulse was 100 the other morning, and it's been in the 70s; 70s mean you're in shape. Being 100 reminds me of how out of shape I am. I looked at myself in the mirror today. I started crying. I look so wide! My bones are gone. I look so filled out! Fat, I guess. I'm scared to wear regular clothes, so I've been going to brunch and therapeutic breakfast in sweats.

I want so much to let this go, but I still hold on so tight. I
say I want to give this up, but there's this voice that says, "I
don't want to weigh 100 pounds." That's how much I
weighed to start with, and I must not like it. I try to trust
you that you won't make me fat. I look at myself, and that's
what I see.

As the struggle continued, she began to become aware of her emotions and feelings and began to notice the value she placed on different
emotions:

I felt really lonely and out of it most of the day. I watched
some of the kids playing around and walking outside. I hear
them laughing and going anywhere they want to. I want to
do that! I want to go outside for a walk. I want to feel like a
part of everyone. I guess I miss living. I want to like where I
am in weight after I get off tubes and the water goes away.
Right now I feel like a balloon and am not happy. Feeling
like this makes me want to go back to being really thin. I
guess I have to trust you. I just want to be happy. Please
don't let me down.

Although her struggle to surrender continued, she began sorting
through her feelings about her weight, herself, and her acceptance by others:

I feel really frustrated. I don't know where I am. I'm in the
middle. I want to give this up, because I am sick of it running my life. I'm having my doubts. I've been in the same
place for months. I don't want to go back, but going up is
just as scary. Thin was me. What's out there? I know there's
something. I feel kind of scared of finding out. I have to feel
proud of something ele. I'm not as scared to eat anymore,
and I don't feel as guilty, depending on how I feel. But I am
doing better about facing it; not about wanting to eat,
though. I do enjoy it more. I just feel depressed, I think
from confusion. This isn't life! I want to go home and enjoy
life, school, friends, and everything, and not worry about
when and what not to eat, and not exercise excessively. I
would like to see what I can do on my own, and what it is
like. When I came in, I never really knew, and I didn't want
to. I want to try, and this gave me a start.

She began to become aware of a decision to relinquish the old
values assigned to elements of the struggle with her body image, and she

was taken off NGTF. She continued to struggle with surrender of old values about weight, thinness, and happiness, but also continued to sort through these feelings and reassign new values.

During the next week she remained in phase 2, the surrender, with emphasis on sorting through her internal awareness of the physical and emotional changes that had taken place during tube feeding. She became increasingly aware of a change in the values she assigned regarding this struggle. The following excerpt summarizes this process and illustrates the close of phase 2 and the initiation of phase 3, hope:

> It's not fair! I feel like whenever I do well, I'm still restricted! I never get to do anything! For six weeks I haven't been able to do anything! Other people here are losing weight, not gaining, and they get walks, meal tickets, or passes. I don't even know if I'm gaining or losing! I don't try to lose. I don't want to. I'm learning to accept this weight. I think I look better. I'm scared to death to gain, though! I'm eating, but those feelings are still there, and they increase. If I walk, it helps me to think, and not exercise in my room. I feel hopeless. I do pretty good, and I'm still restricted. Am I just not ready, or what? I'm sick of doing all this. I want to be happy. But I haven't found a way to start it. My weight is up, I'm trying, but I don't get anywhere. I'm frustrated. I just wanted to give up and go home. Who cares if I'm ano-rectic? But I can't do that. I don't really want to give up! There has to be hope! I don't want to be like this. I want a chance to find out if I can and want to give this up—really want to. I have to find out if I can do it. If not, I'll accept that I'm not ready. But six weeks of nothing—I feel like there's no hope for me. I don't like feeling like that. Am I just hopeless?

This final phase of surrender can be seen again, even more sharply, in the following excerpt:

> I'm frustrated. Is it because I'm trying too hard, or not enough? I want to go somewhere. I feel like I do the same thing every day—eat and sit, and I panic. I don't know what's wrong, so I can't keep still. I hate it. I don't want to go back. I am accepting my weight. I don't want to lose weight. I'm getting scared again. I want to do something else; something con-structive, instead of destructive. I'm not going to be sitting when I get home. I want to walk. I know it wouldn't make me feel as guilty or as panicked. I don't understand me. I want to

try. I do want to get better. I feel like I do. But I feel like I'm sliding. I don't want to. I need some guidance.

She began receiving privileges for additional activity, in accordance with the stability of her weight. Privileges were given gradually, beginning with off-unit privileges and then allowing progressively lengthier walks every day. Weight fluctuations were monitored rather carefully at this phase. She was reminded by the nutritionist of the necessity to implement her eating while being reassured that she was not getting fat. The other patients served as testimonials that they themselves were not getting fat, and that the patient was not at all even near her expected weight range.

Phase 3—hope—began to become more evident, as her writings more freely reflected the new values she had assigned to her issues of struggle with weight. She continued to struggle at this point, with a redefinition of her own identity:

Some mornings I wake up accepting myself and my weight. Sometimes I can look in the mirror and not think I look fat. I feel guilty for feeling that, and I don't want to. I feel guilty for feeling good, because a lot of people here are at rock bottom. It's hard to explain, but I can see the hope most of the time, and they can't, and I want so much to help, but I can't. Then I have to tell myself, I can't go back—I have to keep fighting and help them and support and love them, but not be dragged down. I want to feel okay about myself. I don't want to feel guilty for everything I do. Maybe I'm scared to be an outcast and lonely, rejected by people. But with this, I made an outcast of myself, no matter how much I didn't want to. Why did I do this to myself? I've got most of my eating and exercising under control; it's mainly mental now. I still have some foods that I can't eat. Sometimes I feel fat, but I'm not obsessed with the fatness. I don't think I am. I feel pretty good about my body, better anyway. I'm just having problems with emotions. I guess that'll take a while, though. I figured if people like me for what I weigh, they're not worth it. I keep trying to remind myself of it. I enjoy my meals more. I realize you have to eat. I admitted something today about my exercising and hunger. I feel sometimes that if I don't exercise, then I don't deserve to be hungry. If I'm hungry without exercising, then I won't admit the hunger.

Phase 3 is an evolving one. She continued to reflect on her surrender but began to define her tools to maintain the progress she had realized, both physically and emotionally:

I could really set myself up for a downfall. I have to remember I still have anorexia and probably will for a long time. I'll get it under control, but it's not going to disappear just like that.

I don't know when it started, or how, but I felt fantastic today! I felt good about myself and about how far I've come. I talked a lot today in our group. It was positive. I realized a lot about myself. The only way I can be happy is if I'm happy with myself—inside and outside. I realized that when I go home, I have to do it myself. I'll need support and stuff, and talking things out, but I have to still work in myself. I'll always have to be learning, never shut the doors. If I run into problems, pick myself up. I saw happiness and life today! I don't know how to tell you everything that went through my mind today. I guess I just accepted myself. This is me! I have to live with me for the rest of my life, and I guess I'm not that bad. It was worth all the pain I went through here. I know it's not all over, but I think the hardest part is. I realized I had a problem. I needed help, and I came to the best place to receive it. I've learned so much, not only about anorexia, but also about what I've been missing in my life. I was not happy, but I acted like I was. I didn't feel anything inside. Now I can feel. Anger is great! Happiness, hurt, sadness, thoughtfulness, love! It feels so good to feel again! I know that just because I feel like this today, it doesn't mean I will tomorrow, but having days like this makes me feel like it is all worthwhile.

An upsetting experience occurred during her hospitalization—the return of the menses. The patient, as many patients suffering from eating disorders do, interpreted this event as a return to the obesity she so much loathed. She managed to exercise and restrict sufficiently to lose two kilograms in a week. She was reacquainted with the possibility of NGTF (as a remote possibility) by our simply firing the "salvo" of the scrubs that preceded the tube feeding and having the nutritional support team assess her for NGTF.

In the following ten days, the patient, on her own, regained her weight and remained for only two days on the restricted list and on scrubs. On follow-up, the patient maintained a steady weight, as many anorectics do for some time after discharge. Her general attitude and deportment, however, were better, and the patient considered NGTF a positive experience.

98

Summary and Conclusion

Utilizing the notes written by a patient managed in our program on NGTF, we have illustrated three major components of nutritional rehabilitation. First, we have stressed the necessity of the interpersonal elements applied in this method. Second, we have emphasized the relevance of theoretical frameworks to follow the process. Third, we have provided an analysis of the patient's progress within the theoretical framework. This illustrates the patient's progress through the phases while on NGTF and during the remainder of the nutritional rehabilitation process. If used in this manner, NGTF can become one more important tool in the management of eating-disorder patients.

References

Andersen, A. E. "Treatment of Anorexia Nervosa and Bulimia." In T. Bayless (ed.), *Current Therapy in Gastroenterology.* New York: Decker, 1984.

Andersen, A. E., Morse, C., and Santmyer, K. "Inpatient Treatment for Anorexia Nervosa." In D. M. Garner and P. E. Garfinkel (eds.), *Handbook of Psychotherapy for Anorexia Nervosa and Bulimia.* New York: Guilford Press, 1985.

Bruch, H. *Eating Disorders: Obesity, Anorexia Nervosa, and the Person Within.* New York: Basic Books, 1973.

Green, M., and Greene, H. (eds.). *The Role of the Gastrointestinal Tract in Nutrient Delivery.* New York: Academic Press, 1984.

Halmi, K. "The Diagnosis and Treatment of Anorexia Nervosa." In M. Zales, (ed.), *Eating, Sleeping, and Sexuality: Treatment of Disorders in Basic Life Functions.* New York: Brunner/Mazel, 1982.

Herzog, D. B., and Copeland, P. M. "Eating Disorders." *New England Journal of Medicine,* 1985, *313* (5), 295–303.

Krause, M., and Mahan, L. *Food, Nutrition, and Diet Therapy.* Philadelphia: W.B. Saunders, 1984.

Larocca, F.E.F. "An Inpatient Model for the Treatment of Eating Disorders." *Psychiatric Clinics of North America,* 1984, 7 (2), 287–298.

Vandereycken, W., and Meermann, R. *Anorexia Nervosa: A Clinician's Guide to Treatment.* New York: Walter de Gruyter, 1984.

Félix E. F. Larocca is medical director of the BASH (Bulimia Anorexia Self-Help) Treatment and Research Center at Deaconess Hospital in St. Louis, Missouri, and president and founder of BASH, Inc., in St. Louis, Missouri.

Sherry A. Goodner is BASH community resource and research assistant at Deaconess Hospital in St. Louis, Missouri.

A new approach based on psychodynamic theory explores the use of ego states to explain causation as well as outline a treatment approach for eating disorders.

Psychodynamic Ego-State Therapy for Eating Disorders

Moshe S. Torem

A recent report by Garner and Garfinkel (1985) showed an increase in the prevalence of Anorexia Nervosa in the last ten years, which now is approaching one severe case among every 200 adolescent women. The number of patients with bulimia also appears to be increasing. A recent study by Halmi and others (1981) shows that about 13 percent of the college-age population (19 percent females and 5 percent males) has distorted body images, reports feeling fat regardless of weight, and desires to have much lower weight than what is sound. Although many studies have been published regarding these conditions, their etiology remains obscure and their treatment remains controversial and less than satisfactory (Larocca, 1984; Mitchell, 1985; Brotman and others, 1984; Pope and others, 1983; Moor and Rakes, 1982; Wermuth and others, 1977; Long and Cordle, 1982; Garner and Bemis, 1985; Stevens and Salisbury, 1984).

The psychodynamic point of view subscribes to the idea that all mental phenomena are the result of an interaction of forces. Freud described throughout his writings the major forces of this struggle and repeatedly emphasized the concept of psychic determinism or causality, according to which mental phenomena, as well as behaviors, are not chance occurrences but are meaningfully related to events that preceded them; unless made conscious, they will be subject to repetition. As these

F.E.F. Larocca (ed.). *Eating Disorders.*
New Directions for Mental Health Services, no. 31. San Francisco: Jossey-Bass, Fall 1986.

issues relate to patients with eating disorders, it is conceptualized that the patient with Anorexia Nervosa and the patient with bulimia manifest symptoms that are the expression of unresolved, subconscious, intrapsychic conflicts. The patient with Anorexia Nervosa has been viewed as having the illness as a result of an underlying mechanism to deny and defend against assuming the female sexual role. There is an exaggerated awareness and focus on the patient's bodily needs, and thus there is an avoidance of the underlying psychological conflicts. In patients with anorexia and bulimia, we can also view their condition as a phobic and obsessive-compulsive reaction to underlying, unrecognized anxiety and anger. For many young women, it has been stated that the development of an eating disorder serves as a self-punishing mechanism to alleviate a sense of guilt associated with the expression of unacceptable feelings and conflicts.

The above has been a rather typical psychodynamic explanation found in the literature for patients with eating disorders. However, the typical, classical, psychoanalytic approaches have produced rather poor results in the treatment of these patients.

This chapter describes a new approach to the treatment of eating disorder, called here *psychodynamic ego-state therapy* and based on the notion that human behavior is not always consistent but shows a great variety at different times. I propose to explain and describe psychodynamic ego-state therapy, for the treatment of patients with eating disorders.

The Concept of Ego States

Paul Federn (1953) was the first to formulate the concept of ego states. Federn, who was a close associate of Freud, formulated the concept of ego states as an organized entity of the ego. He said that these ego states were separated by boundaries that were more or less permeable and perceived themselves as the subject "I." The term *ego state* has been used by a number of writers, such as Berne (1961), who described in detail the concept of transactional analysis; Hartmann (1958); Kohut (1971); and Watkins and Watkins (1979).

Watkins and Watkins defined an ego state as an organized system of behavior and experience whose elements are bound together by some common principle but are separated from one another by boundaries that are more or less permeable. They also continued to conceptualize each ego state to constitute a kind of subself, which has more or less individual autonomy in relation to other states and to the entire personality. For the purpose of adaptation, these ego states, which represent different cognitions, perceptions, affects, and behaviors, are partially dissociated from each other. However, the boundaries are permeable. Separation among the various ego states occurs via the mechanism of dissociation, which can be very mild, whereby there are very flexible boundaries among the various ego states. However, at the other end of the continuum, the boundaries among the various ego states can be rigid and relatively impermeable. This may be manifested by multiple personalities, with possible amnesia and conflict among the various ego states.

Watkins (1978) describes the separation of ego states as a relative dissociation determined by a degree of rigidity and permeability of boundaries among the various ego states. Dissociation, according to Watkins, lies on a continuum. In healthy dissociation, we may see a father who, in one ego state, may crawl on the floor with his child, while shortly after that he is on the phone giving sophisticated instructions to an emergency room nurse on how to manage a medical crisis. On the other end of the continuum, we have the person with a multiple-personality disorder. In between, a wide range of personality organizations and structures may exist.

Ego states can be activated by the use of hypnotic and nonhypnotic techniques. When an ego state is activated, it views itself as the subject "I" and experiences other ego states and views the rest of the individual as the objects "he," "she," or "it." The ego state that is primary at any given moment is conceptualized as the "executive." For that moment, it is considered the self. Ego states can function together in relative harmony. Disagreements are resolved through internal dialogue and mutual recognition of various conflicting needs, interests, and desires. Finally, a decision is made through compromise, with recognition of the demands and limitations of reality and the possible consequences of future behavior. However, when the boundaries among ego states are relatively nonpermeable, disharmony may occur, whereby one ego state gets involved in actions and behaviors that may be in great conflict with other ego states or with the entire individual. In such a case, ego states function with relatively high autonomy and little consideration for the needs of the entire individual. This may create severe internal conflict and become a prominent factor in such maladaptive phenomena as overeating, binge-purging, self-starvation, excessive exercising, headaches, and many other emotional and physical symptoms.

According to Watkins and Watkins, ego states usually stem from one of three sources:

(1) They may split off at the time of a great trauma and serve as a defense for the individual going through the trauma (Watkins, 1976). An unhappy condition may serve to initiate such a split of a new ego state, as well as a specific trauma. Lonely children often create imaginary companions and, in most cases, these latter disappear as other social experiences fulfill the lonely child's needs and prevent the loneliness. Years later, through the use of hypnosis, the ego state of an imaginary playmate can be activated and can describe the exact condition under which it was orig-

inally created. It can also describe its continuous role in subconsciously influencing the patient's present behavior.

(2) Ego states may be built around parental introjects, but the child may also introject the conflictual drama of his interaction with the parents or with other family members. It is important to note that any introjection of an external object or event represents the child's perception of the external reality, be it pleasant, loving, or hostile. The activation of an introjected ego state results in being faced with an ego state that thinks and feels as a child does. The younger the age of the child when the introjection occurs, the more primitive and infantile will be the introjected ego state.

(3) Ego states may be created through normal development. The self is being conceptualized as a society of ego states, which consists of various clusters, of behaviors and experiences that may be partially dissociated from one another through semipermeable boundaries. This allows the individual to focus on each particular daily situation adaptively, with minimal interference from nonrelevant elements of the personality. Ego states will express such thoughts as "I am the one who makes him a good father" or "It is my job to see that he is a good student" or "I make sure that he always shows up on time for work" or "I keep him alert and protect him from falling asleep on duty."

Hilgard (1973, 1977) discovered that subjects who had been rendered hypnotically deaf or whose hands had been anesthetized under hypnosis were hearing and sensing pain at levels below the threshold of normal awareness. Hilgard described this phenomenon as a cognitive, structural state of mind and termed it "the Hidden Observer." "The Hidden Observers" are the same phenomena as those ego states described by Watkins and Watkins.

Eating Disorders Resulting from Conflicted Ego States

Anorexia Nervosa and bulimia are sometimes best understood as results of conflicts among disharmonious ego states fighting for executive control. Early in the screening process, listening carefully to patients' statements is of great benefit: "I sometimes do not know why I do it. I am so confused. It is not like me." "A part of me wants to binge and then throw up, and another part of me hates it and is just plain disgusted." "Whenever food is put in front of me, I automatically become frightened, like a little kid. I know I need to eat, but it is as if the devil gets into me." "When I binge, it feels so strange, as if I am in a daze. I don't know what comes over me."

In screening and assessment, patients with underlying dissociation mechanisms for their disorders will be the best candidates for ego-state therapy.

Ego-State Therapy

Ego-state therapy is defined by the Watkins and Watkins (1982) as "the utilization of family and group treatment techniques for the resolution of conflicts between the different ego states, which constitute a 'family of self' within a single individual." This method is aimed at conflict resolution and may employ directive, behavioral, psychoanalytical, supportive, existential, and even relaxation or biofeedback techniques of therapy. This mode of therapy is concerned with the notion of how much the individual's behavior is the result of dissociated ego states with rigid, nonflexible boundaries.

The experience of ego-state therapy shows that activating, studying, and communicating with various ego states does not increase the patient's tendency to dissociate. On the contrary, the patient who used to dissociate, and for whom an ego state switched the executive control, experienced many of these changes as mood swings, confusion states, lost time, and so on. When the patient developed an awareness of his condition, confusion was replaced by greater clarity, understanding, new hope, and a sense of self-mastery. The goal of ego-state therapy is not total fusion of all ego states, but rather an increased permeability of ego-state boundaries and improved internal harmony, resulting in better cooperation and congruence among the various ego states. Ego states may be maladaptive; however, the strategy is not to eliminate any ego state, even if it is responsible for maladaptive behavior. Instead, the strategy is to change the maladaptive behavior and make the ego state more adaptive in its behavior. The following is a detailed description of the steps involved in doing ego-state therapy.

The Activation of Ego States

Ego states can be activated by the use of hypnotic and nonhypnotic techniques. With nonhypnotic techniques, any number of methods of therapy can be used. The Gestalt technique using the empty chair and switching from one chair to another, based on the ego state identified as responsible for the specific behavior, is one example. Another method is called the "personal diary technique," whereby patients are instructed to keep personal diaries and write in them every day, reflecting on thoughts, feelings, and behavior regarding eating, the relationship with the therapist, past events as they come to mind, and future plans. Patients are then instructed to sign their names at the end of each entry. Many patients respond very favorably to this technique, expressing surprise that the doctor is interested in reading and listening to the patient's writings.

Some patients disclose that they have been writing for years and have personal diaries describing their feelings, thoughts, and reflections as they relate to the daily emotional turmoil and confusion that they have been going through. In examining the diary, the therapist looks for changes in the patient's handwriting, signature, and name. Sometimes there is a significant difference in the patient's handwriting, depending on the mood or the ego state responsible for the binge-purge behavior, dieting, or excessive exercising.

Ego states can also be activated by the use of hypnotic techniques. Using hypnosis saves time and involves procedures taking from one to three minutes. The patient is examined for hypnotizability, using the Hypnotic Induction Profile (Spiegel and Bridger, 1970). If the patient is found to have a capacity for hypnosis, he or she is guided into a hypnotic trance after proper instruction in self-hypnosis, which usually takes five minutes. Then a hypnoanalytic technique is used, whereby the patient is asked about the ego state responsible for the binge-purge behavior or the self-starvation behavior. That particular ego state is then invited to communicate directly with the therapist. Sometimes there is initial resistance to oral communication. If this happens, options are given to communicate either in writing or through the host ego state, and assurance is given that each ego state will be treated with respect and dignity.

Therapeutic Communication with Hidden Ego States

Communicating with the ego state responsible for a patient's abnormal eating behavior is done not only to identify that ego state but also to find out the reasons for this behavior. It is important to follow the principle of separating the pattern of the actual behavior (bingeing, purging, or dieting) from the underlying intention. This opens up a deeper level of choice for the desired change to take place.

After some discussion, in which the distinction between the behavior pattern and the positive purpose behind it is clarified, the communication must move toward convincing the ego state to take on new, alternative behaviors, of higher adaptive quality, to replace the older ones. These new patterns of behavior will still serve the old intention, but the destructive, maladaptive elements (bingeing, purging, or excessive dieting) will be replaced by behavior that is adaptive and age-appropriate, as well as satisfying.

In the case of patients with eating disorders, abnormal eating behavior is replaced by age-appropriate ways of expressing anger, obtaining and experiencing joy, or letting go of guilt feelings through charitable acts of helping others, rather than by self-punishment. It takes special creative skills in communicating, negotiating, and mediating to persuade resistant ego states to change their patterns of behavior. Many times the patient is given the suggestion to do this for the sake of the whole. This suggestion communicates the message that ego states do not exist in a vacuum but are part of the whole person. Any behavior by an ego state must take into account the consequences for the other ego states and, of course, for the patient as a whole.

Ratification

The ego state that produced the undesirable eating behavior (the symptom) is the one that is expected to be responsible for initiating the new, adaptive pattern of behavior (the cure). Once the patient has considered a new, adaptive way to cope and serve the old purpose, the doctor may give the patient a behavioral "homework" assignment, first to write about the new behavior and then to practice it. Such direct assignments are not used in psychoanalysis; however, it is implied that behavioral change in the patient will take place, and that the patient is to initiate it.

Ecological Check

Although an ego state responsible for abnormal eating may have agreed to change its pattern, the patient's entire system needs to be examined. If this is not done, the change in behavior may be what some psychoanalysts have termed an *ego-alien change.* This may happen if other components of the patient's personality demand the return of the abnormal eating behaviors, even when the ego state that originally produced it is willing to let it go. Such resistance to change may originate from secondary gain. This must be addressed and is done in psychotherapy by using the working-through process, by careful examination, clarification, confrontation, and repeated suggestions for change.

The therapeutic communication methods for ego states that have been discussed here are based on the reframing model elaborated by Bandler (1978). The model includes seven steps:

1. Identify the abnormal eating behavior that needs to be changed.
2. Identify the ego state responsible for the abnormal eating pattern.
3. Establish communication with the responsible ego state.
4. Separate pattern from intention.
5. Negotiate with the responsible ego state to replace the old pattern with a new pattern of behavior that is age-appropriate to the individual in the present reality and that satisfies the original intention.
6. Ratify the new behavioral pattern with the responsible ego state.
7. Conduct an ecological review of the entire system to confirm the acceptance of the new behavioral pattern and get commitment for action.

The goals of ego-state therapy for patients with eating disorders are change in eating behavior, replacing abnormal eating patterns with healthy behavior; freedom from obsessive preoccupation with food; and relief from body-image distortion. All these goals can be accomplished by allowing for greater permeability and flexibility of ego-state boundaries, eliminating dissociative amnesias, and creating a state of greater internal harmony.

References

Bandler, L. C. *They Lived Happily Ever After.* Cupertino, Calif.: Meta Publications, 1978.

Berne, E. *Transactional Analysis in Psychotherapy.* New York: Grove Press, 1961.

Brotman, A. W., Herzog, D. B., and Woods, S. W. "Antidepressant Treatment of Bulimia: The Relationship Between Bingeing and Depressive Symptomatology." *Journal of Clinical Psychiatry,* 1984, *45,* 7–9.

Federn, P. *Ego Psychology and the Psychoses.* London: Imago, 1953.

Garner, D. M., and Bemis, K. M. "Cognitive Therapy for Anorexia Nervosa." In D. M. Garner and P. E. Garfinkel (eds.), *Handbook of Psychotherapy for Anorexia Nervosa and Bulimia.* New York: Guilford Press, 1985.

Garner, D. M., and Garfinkel, P. E. (eds.). *Handbook of Psychotherapy for Anorexia Nervosa and Bulimia.* New York: Guilford Press, 1985.

Halmi, K. A., Falk, J. R., and Schwartz, E. "Binge-Eating and Vomiting: A Survey of a College Population." *Psychological Medicine,* 1981, *11,* 697–706.

Hartmann, H. *Ego Psychology and the Problems of Adaptation.* New York: International University Press, 1958.

Hilgard, E. R. "Dissociation Revisited." In M. Henle, J. Jaynes, and J. Sullivan (eds.), *Historical Conceptions of Psychology.* New York: Springer, 1973.

Hilgard, E. R. *Divided Consciousness: Multiple Controls in Human Thoughts and Actions.* New York: Wiley, 1977.

Kohut, H. *The Analysis of the Self.* New York: International Universities Press, 1971.

Larocca, F.E.F. "An Inpatient Model for the Treatment of Eating Disorders." *Psychiatric Clinics of North America,* 1984, *7* (2), 287–298.

Long, C. G., and Cordle, C. J. "Psychological Treatment of Binge Eating and Self-Induced Vomiting." *British Journal of Medical Psychology,* 1982, *55,* 139–145.

Mitchell, J. E. (ed.). *Anorexia Nervosa and Bulimia: Diagnosis and Treatment.* Minneapolis: University of Minnesota Press, 1985.

Moor, S. L., and Rakes, S. M. "Binge-Eating: Therapeutic Response to Diphenyl-hydantoin: Case Report." *Journal of Clinical Psychiatry,* 1982, *43,* 385–386.

Pope, H. G., Jr., Hudson, J. I., Jonas, J. M., and Yurgelun-Todd, D. "Bulimia Treated with Imipramine: A Placebo-Controlled, Double-Blind Study." *American Journal of Psychiatry,* 1983, *140* (5), 554–558.

Spiegel, H., and Bridger, A. A. *Manual for Hypnotic Induction Profile.* New York: Soni Medica, 1970.

Stevens, E. V., and Salisbury, J. D. "Group Therapy for Bulimic Adults." *American Journal of Orthopsychiatry,* 1984, *54,* 156–161.

Watkins, J. G. "Ego States and the Problem of Responsibility: A Psychological Analysis of the Patty Hearst Case." *Science of Psychiatry and the Law,* 1976, 489–491.

Watkins, J. G. *The Therapeutic Self.* New York: Human Sciences Press, 1978.

Watkins, J. G., and Watkins, H. H. "Ego States and Hidden Observers." *Journal of Altered States of Consciousness,* 1979, *5,* 3–18.

Watkins, J. G., and Watkins, H. H. "Ego-State Therapy." In L. E. Abt and J. R. Stuart (eds.), *The Newer Therapies: A Sourcebook.* New York: Von Nostrand Reinhold, 1982.

Wermuth, B. M., Davis, K. L., Hollister, L., and Stunkard, A. J. "Phenytoin Treatment of the Binge-Eating Syndrome." *American Journal of Psychiatry,* 1977, *134,* 1249–1253.

Moshe S. Torem is chairman of the Department of Psychiatry and Behavioral Sciences at Akron General Medical Center and professor of psychiatry, Northeastern Ohio University College of Medicine in Akron, Ohio.

Hypnosis is explored as an alternative treatment approach for patients who are amenable to it.

Use of Hypnosis in Eating Disorders

Meir Gross

Anorexia Nervosa and bulimia are baffling diseases, in which adolescent girls (and rarely males) will starve themselves to death or binge-purge any food consumed. Many treatment modalities have been tried for these severe and debilitating conditions, but only limited success is reported. A mortality rate of up to 20 percent has been quoted (Hsu and others, 1979; Hsu, 1980; Crisp and others, 1976). Therapy with many patients is difficult and complex, because most resist treatment and have difficulties in relinquishing their need for the anorectic symptoms, since these symptoms represent other, underlying conflicts. Many adolescents fear growing up and use anorexia as a means of stopping the process. Some have delayed psychosexual development and cannot cope with the transition during adolescence. Sexual interest declines markedly during the course of the illnesses.

Hypnosis has not been widely used in the treatment of these disorders. The motivation and cooperation of the patient are important factors in successful hypnotherapy. If the patient resists, even the best hypnotherapist may fail in the induction of trance, let alone achieve a therapeutic goal.

Review of the Literature

The first one to describe the use of hypnotherapy for anorexia was Pierre Janet (1925), who called the illness Hysterical Anorexia. He stressed

F.E.F. Larocca (ed.). *Eating Disorders.*
New Directions for Mental Health Services, no. 31. San Francisco: Jossey-Bass, Fall 1986.

that hypnosis was only one part of a more complex therapy. He used hypnosis in patients who were receiving structured supportive therapy in a hospital environment. Brenman and Gill (1947) reported a case of a fourteen-year-old anorectic girl who benefited by the use of hypnosis. The therapeutic suggestions given to her were indirect and were meant to provide a safe and secure environment in order to help her gain weight. This girl was hopping excessively, and so the suggestion was given to reducing the hopping, which indirectly made the patient eat more and regain her strength and normal body weight.

Crasilneck and Hall (1975) also described the use of hypnosis for treating anorexia. They used instructions for self-hypnosis when treating their patients. They suggested increasing awareness of hunger by equating it with the enjoyment of eating. Increasing food intake was only the first step, however. They also recommended hypnoanalysis for uncovering the psychodynamic conflicts underlying the anorectic symptoms. They treated seventy cases of anorexia and achieved marked improvement in more than half. Kroger and Fezler (1976) reported success in combining behavior therapy with hypnosis. Their patients were given posthypnotic suggestions in a direct manner, associating food and good appetite with pleasant memories. They also emphasized the fact that hypnosis often fosters rapport between patient and therapist. The therapist can then use images to enhance feelings of hunger or emptiness in the stomach. For patients who claimed they were unable to eat because of a full feeling in the stomach, they suggested recalling images of past hunger.

Through hypnosis, Thakur (1980) has given suggestions to patients for deeper values in life, better eating habits (including increased food intake for weight gain), altering of the body image into a more realistic perception, and self-assertion in interpersonal relationships.

Spiegel and Spiegel (1978) have reported the value of hypnosis for Anorexia Nervosa, both as an aid to the diagnostic process and later in treatment. Hypnosis has proved helpful in sorting out underlying psychiatric disorders, thus increasing the effectiveness of therapy. Ambrose and Newbold (1980) reported two separate cases of boys who suffered from anorexia but also presented with gender confusion. Suggestions were given to patients to reassure them about their masculinity. These suggestions, directed toward emphasizing male characteristics, produced positive therapeutic results.

Milton Erickson (Erickson and Rossi, 1979) described hypnotherapy of an anorectic fourteen-year-old girl during a month-long intensive treatment. Erickson used indirect suggestions and paradoxical strategies during four phases of the therapy. The first phase used distracting frames of reference, instructing the patient to take better oral hygiene. The second depotentiated masochistic defenses through instructions to the patient to rinse her mouth daily with cod liver oil. The consequence of failure was eating food. The patient, of course, failed and had to eat. The third phase used therapeutic double-blind suggestions as instruction to the patient to oversee her parents' weight gain. The fourth used emotional catharsis by provoking the patient—for instance, by accusing her of being a liar and a coward.

A detailed description of hypnotic treatment of anorectics was presented by Gross (1982). Core symptoms of the illness were identified and were responsive to hypnotherapy, which was augmented by teaching the patients self-hypnosis. These symptoms are presented as follows. Understanding these dynamics is important for better use of hypnotherapy in eating-disorder patients.

The Background of the Anorectic Emerging Symptoms

External precipitating events (divorce or separation of parents, seeing a sibling leave home, having to go away to college, not being popular in school, and so on) overwhelm the growing adolescent girl. Life is not perfect anymore. She cannot cope with growing up and facing the realities of adult life. Loneliness, self-doubt, and poor self-esteem drive the girl into preoccupation with her appearance and physical development. Thoughtless remarks by friends or family members about her "big hips" or "tummy" might induce her to go on destructive diets, so that friends or others important in her life will appreciate her thin body. As the girl begins to lose weight, she feels proud of her will power.

Such girls are perfectionists. The ability to block and ignore hunger is a source of pride, which is reinforced by success in getting thin. Most of these patients report that they feel hungry, but these feelings are effectively suppressed, either by the patients' ignoring them, while busy in a heavy daily schedule, or getting involved in exhausting exercises. The patients usually distort normal feelings of hunger or satiation into feelings of emptiness or fullness. Hunger or satiation stops being the primary physiological regulator of food intake.

Losing weight compensates for feelings of worthlessness or powerlessness and gives a sense of control, which masks feelings of incompetence (Sours, 1969). The need for control becomes so important that the patients are willing to manipulate their environments in order to continue losing weight by any means available—ritualistic behavior about eating, eating slowly, vomiting, or using purgatives, for example. Awareness of hunger becomes confused with abnormal self-evaluation; distorted body image (Bruch, 1962, 1969) is an example of this.

The history of the anorectic patient reveals intense enmeshment with the family. Usually the family is of upper or middle-class origins, well established, and obsessed with achievement and success, regardless of feelings. The parents reward automatic compliance and perfection; "intrusive concern" is typical (Minuchin and others, 1975). These patients not only fail to achieve emotional identity and independence; they are not even in tune with their own bodies.

Normally developing adolescents learn to respond to their own inner cues—something anorectics cannot do. This failure is the central core of their psychopathology. The constant blocking of inner needs results in separation of feelings from thoughts. An obsessive-compulsive personality, governed by perfectionistic fantasies, develops. Perfectionism and the blocking of impulses results in restless overactivity, to the point of exhaustion, and in the inability to relax. Activities are pursued in a driven, obsessive manner. Patients cannot sit still unless they are doing something "useful."

This level of compulsiveness triggers increased sympathetic body tonus, which is evident in relaxation trials with biofeedback equipment. The patient experiences lowering of peristalsis, constipation, a feeling of fullness, and suppression of hunger. Endocrine function is decreased, as seen in the reduction of sexual drive and the amenorrhea typical of Anorexia Nervosa.

On the basis of clinical observations, it can be stated that the goal of successful hypnotherapy should be directed toward alteration of body image and interoception. The patient's difficulties with internal cues should be recognized, and an attempt should be made to sensitize her toward self-awareness. Self-perception helps the patient to become aware of hunger and satiety, and especially of the body's need for relaxation. Therapy should raise the patient's sense of effectiveness and self-esteem. The ability to recognize and accept sexual needs and increase both internal and external perceptions are important goals of therapy.

Identification of Target Symptoms for Hypnotherapy

Overactivity and Tension. The typical overactive anorectic girl needs to realize the level of her own activity. Suggestions for relaxation and slowed respiration and heart rate, combined with pleasurable feelings and soothing imagery, can counteract this overactivity and tension.

Distorted Body Image. Use of tactile stimuli from distorted body parts, and use of photography, showing the patient's own emaciated body and comparing it with a healthy body image, may provide a move toward health.

Defect in Introspective Awareness. Hypnotic suggestions for better attention to visceral cues, especially hunger and satiety, usually improve patient's self-awareness.

Family Enmeshment. Direct suggestion for self-assertion and improved self-esteem helps in the process of separation from the "suffocating" family situation. Hypnotic age progression, like projections into the future, can facilitate self-sufficiency outside the family.

Repressed Traumatic Events. Use of age regression under the hypnotic trance can reveal stress dynamics associated with the onset of the anorectic process.

Resistance to Therapy. Resistance may be overt, covert, or both. Teaching the patient self-hypnosis is a means for better self-control, which includes weight control. Improved vocational or athletic performance can also be an indirect hypnotic suggestion for better care of the body.

Hypnotic Suggestions, with Case Presentations

Suggestions to Counteract Hyperactivity. One of the earliest beneficial effects of hypnotherapy for the anorectic is relaxation. Whether through self-hypnosis or regular sessions with a hypnotherapist, the patient is able to calm her overactive neuromuscular system. Hypnotic relaxation, like the relaxation response described by Beary and Benson (1974), is associated with a generalized decrease in the activity of the sympathetic nervous system. Heartbeat and respiration rate decrease. The electroencephalogram shows slow alpha-wave activity. The patient not only benefits from hypnotic relaxation but can also give some thought to her deepest feelings and goals in life, maybe for the first time.

Case 1

Kelly, a fifteen-year-old girl, was admitted to the hospital in a severe state of emaciation. She had never been able to stay in bed during the day and was always on the go. The high level of energy in this thin, cachectic body was an enigma. An intelligent girl looking for new experiences, she learned self-hypnosis as part of the treatment program. She practiced fifteen minutes a day, and her overactive level of behavior gradually changed. She gained more than 1 kg a week. When asked about her experiences with self-hypnosis, she said that she was able to feel calm, think about herself and the conflicts that made her start dieting, and be in touch with her body and its feelings.

Under hypnosis, she was led to envision herself in a beautiful setting, such as a park or the beach.

The patient finally realized that stimuli (whether internal or external) can be pleasurable and should be sought and enjoyed.

Suggestions for Correcting Body Image. The anorectic patient has a notoriously distorted body image. To help her realize this, the hypnotized patient is shown photographs of her emaciated body, and a healthier body image is then suggested. Asking the patient to draw pictures of herself is also instructive. Often she will draw a normal torso but attach it to hugely distorted hips. Once the therapist realizes that only part of the body image is distorted, he or she can concentrate primarily on that portion. During trance, the patient is asked to touch each part of her body, including the stomach and the heart, and especially the most distorted parts. After a time, the patient comes to understand that her conception of that part of her anatomy is not real.

Case 2

Cathy, seventeen, began dieting after her boyfriend mentioned that she had big thighs. When admitted to the hospital, she had gone from 59 to 36.4 kg.

She was taught self-hypnosis and was asked to concentrate on the photograph of herself taken on hospital admission. She was then instructed to view the picture of her body and to visualize a projected future image of herself, perhaps modeled after the image of a favorite movie star. Gradually, she gained a more realistic perception of her body and began increasing her food intake.

Suggestions for Correcting Defects in Interoceptive Awareness. The anorectic has no perception of sensations, especially hunger, from her own internal organs. Because of this, she cannot even perceive the sensation of satiety, and when hunger can no longer be blocked, she will eat huge amounts of food without being able to stop. Vomiting becomes an artificial means of control, and the use of laxatives becomes an everyday measure of reducing. Hypnosis can help unblock these sensations.

Case 3

Brenda, eighteen, lost 12.3 kg (down from only 46.5 kg) after someone remarked that she was a "fatso." She would starve herself for a few days and then give up and gorge herself on anything available.

Guilt would follow, which she got rid of by including vomiting with her finger and then swallowing a large quantity of laxatives. During trance, Brenda was advised to concentrate on feeling hungry and to respond by eating a small amount of food, to the point of feeling satisfied. Later she was able to increase her regular food intake and reach her goal of 45.3 kg without resorting to vomiting or laxative abuse.

Suggestions for Separation from the Family and Better Sense of Effectiveness. Most anorectics lack self-esteem. Given their perfectionism, anything they do seems unsuccessful and not good enough. This is the main reason most of them also suffer depression.

Case 4

Marion, fifteen, had been an active girl before she went from 65 to 35.4 kg. During her evaluation, it was found that her parents were on the verge of separation. They angrily refused any suggestion of family therapy.

By starving herself, she gained some control over her parents, who forgot their animosities long enough to evince some concern about her.

Self-hypnosis enabled her to regain some proper sense of control. Projection into the future during trance helped her to separate herself emotionally from her parents and seek control over her own life, rather than over theirs. She regained her weight and became more assertive, and her self-esteem rose.

Suggestions. "See yourself as you would like to be five or ten years from now. Realize how independent and self-sufficient you can be with complete control over your life, completely by yourself, away from your family's problems." Such suggestions enabled Marion to gain control over her future, even though she felt helpless about the present family situation.

Use of Hypnosis as a Tool for Abreaction of Repressed Traumatic Events

Sometimes a traumatic event is the source of anorexia. Early trauma, not discussed during regular sessions, may be revealed during hypnotic age regression. Recognition of this childhood event and working through the abreacted feelings can lead to successful resolution of anorexia.

Case 5

Ruth, twenty-three, had suffered from Anorexia Nervosa for eight years. Eighteen months of intensive psychotherapy four years previously had resulted in some weight gain, but she stopped eating as soon as therapy ended. She was willing to try hypnosis; traditional psychotherapy had not helped her.

Under hypnosis, she was age-regressed to fifteen years, about the time the anorexia had begun. During trance, she abreacted her feelings by crying and reliving her depression. At traditional psychotherapy, she had denied these feelings altogether.

Suggestions. "Now you are watching the movie of your life, going backwards from the present time to your childhood. If you see anything upsetting, raise your right finger. I will stop the movie, and you can tell me about it." If the event is too traumatic, the therapist can remind the patient that it is only a movie.

By four months, her weight has risen to 55 kg and was maintained steadily during more than two years of follow-up.

Use of Hypnosis to Overcome Resistance

As already mentioned, one of the major difficulties in psychotherapy of anorectic patients is overt or covert resistance. At the very beginning of therapy, the patient will object to any pressure to increase food intake, and direct suggestions may actually antagonize her. When hypnotherapy is offered as a weight-control tool, it is often accepted. Properly presented, self-hypnosis will pose no threat to the patient's personal sovereignty, since it is now seen as a means of gaining further control over herself.

A knowledgeable therapist can seize on something important to the patient to introduce self-hypnosis and at the same time indirectly suggest better eating habits, in order to improve her performance—for example, in tennis. The therapist can emphasize that in self-hypnosis the patient will gain complete control, and that even in heterohypnosis the operator does not control the subject.

Case 6

Regina, twenty-seven, had been treated by three psychiatrists over a twelve-year period but continued to lose weight. At twenty-seven, her weight had dropped to 32 kg. She resisted anything that might make her "fat." Hypnotherapy was suggested.

In about four months, her weight had returned to about 55 kg and was retained successfully.

The Hypnotherapeutic Suggestions for Bulimia

Almost 50 percent of anorectic patients also suffer from bulimia. The following are hypnotic suggestions given to patients that enable them to have better control of eating and to avoid binges that lead to the self-induced vomiting or laxative abuse typical in bulimia.

First Suggestions. "Never skip any meal. Eat three meals every day. If you are concerned about how many calories you consume for the whole day, you can eat minimal amounts at each meal, so that the whole daily amount will fit your dietary calculations. Skipping meals or starving for the whole day will cause low blood sugar, or hypoglycemia, and could bring cold sweat, the feeling of fainting, and a voracious appetite. At the point of hypoglycemia, you probably cannot avoid bingeing, even if you tell yourself you will eat only small amounts. Unfortunately, the physiological effect of low blood sugar overcomes your best intentions to eat only a small meal. Of course, you will get mad at yourself for bingeing, even if it is not your fault. You go directly to the bathroom to do your routine of getting rid of the food. What do you think happens? You deplete your body of the available sugar, remain in a state of low blood sugar, and then you binge again, with starches, carbohydrates, sugar, and junk food. What follows then? You bet: no need for guessing."

The conclusion is that skipping meals only leads to the vicious cycle of bingeing and purging, with no end to it unless the patient accepts the hypnotic suggestion to eat three meals a day.

Second Suggestion. "Find other ways to keep your weight steady—like keeping to a good, balanced diet. There are people who turn to bulimia as an easy way to lose weight or keep their weight down. Of course, it is more difficult to observe a diet strictly. Many people are also confused about the many diets available. You may get tired of following each diet. You could keep your weight down by just following one rule of thumb: Eat mainly vegetables, cooked or raw, as in salads. They have a lot of roughage in them and are low in calories. Fruits are good for the same reason. In addition, stick to high-protein foods like seafood, chicken (without the fat), lean meats, eggs, and low-fat milk products, which are also rich in proteins and nutrients. Avoid eating carbohydrates like cakes, cookies, sweets, and chocolates. Eat minimal amounts of bread and noodles. If you are eating a lot of carbohydrates, the insulin in your body will lower your blood sugar even more than normally, causing low blood sugar, which could trigger a bingeing episode and start a bulimic cycle. If you want to follow a diet of your choice, you can suggest to yourself to stick to this diet."

Third Suggestion. "One of the best secrets of nature for losing weight and stabilizing it at a normal, healthy level is the use of proper exercise. Jogging, jumping rope, and swimming are effective methods. They can be quite enjoyable, if they are done together with others. They could become enjoyable social events."

Fourth Suggestion. "The way you eat is important in controlling your weight. Obese people usually tend to eat fast and therefore consume higher amounts of food before they feel satiated, because of the time it takes for the food to be absorbed and the message to reach the satiety center. This is estimated to be up to fifteen or twenty minutes. If you eat slowly, you let the food be absorbed, and you get the message from the satiety center that you are full before you even finish your plate. If you eat fast, you may eat two or three times more than you need before you get the feeling of satiety.

"It is also good advice to drink a cup of water, a diet drink, coffee, or tea without sugar before each meal. The liquid will partially fill your stomach before you start to eat, and the small amount you eat slowly will mix better in your stomach and be absorbed better and faster. That way, you get the message from the satiety center earlier. Making it a point to have the no-calorie drink before each meal helps you stabilize your weight by helping you avoid eating too much or bingeing."

The major factor in successful hypnotherapy is the degree of the patient's motivation. Like alcoholics, who will get motivated only after getting to the lowest points in their lives, anorectics or bulimics often have to reach their own low points in order to start kicking the habit. The higher the motivation, the better the prognosis. Patients who are motivated will be eager to learn self-hypnosis and face the responsibilities of quitting

118

their addictive behaviors of bingeing and purging. They will be able to cure themselves. The same is true in Anorexia Nervosa. Only when patients are eager to take care of their bodies will hypnosis succeed.

References

Ambrose, G., and Newbold, G. *A Handbook of Medical Hypnosis*. London: Bailliere Tindale, 1980.

Beary, J. F., and Benson, H. "A Simple Psychophysiologic Technique Which Elicits the Hypometabolic Changes of the Relaxation Response." *Psychosomatic Medicine*, 1974, *36*, 115-120.

Brenman, M., and Gill, M. *Hypnotherapy*. New York: International Universities Press, 1947.

Bruch, H. "Perceptual and Conceptual Disturbances in Anorexia Nervosa." *Psychosomatic Medicine*, 1962, *24*, 187-194.

Bruch, H. "Hunger and Instinct." *Journal of Nervous and Mental Disorders*, 1969, *149*, 91-114.

Crasilneck, H. B., and Hall, J. A. *Clinical Hypnosis: Principles and Applications*. New York: Grune & Stratton, 1975.

Crisp, A. H., Palmer, R. L., and Kalucy, R. S. "How Common Is Anorexia Nervosa? A Prevalence Study." *British Journal of Psychiatry*, 1976, *128*, 549-554.

Erickson, M., and Rossi, E. *Hypnotherapy: An Exploratory Casebook*. New York: Irvington, 1979.

Gross, M. *Anorexia Nervosa: A Comprehensive Approach*. Lexington, Mass.: The Collamore Press, 1982.

Hsu, L.K.G. "Outcome of Anorexia Nervosa: A Review of the Literature (1954-1978)." *Archives of General Psychiatry*, 1980, *37*, 1041-1046.

Hsu, L.K.G., Crisp, A. H., and Harding, B. "Outcome of Anorexia Nervosa." *Lancet*, 1979, *1*, 61-65.

Janet, P. *Psychological Healing*. Vol. 2. New York: Macmillan, 1925.

Kroger, W. S., and Fezler, W. D. *Hypnosis and Behavior Modification: Imagery Conditioning*. Philadelphia: Lippincott, 1976.

Minuchin, S., Baker, L., Rosman, B. L., Liebman, R., Milan, L., and Todd, T. D. "A Conceptual Model of Psychosomatic Illness in Children, Family Organization and Family Therapy." *Archives of General Psychiatry*, 1975, *32*, 1031-1038.

Sours, J. A. "Anorexia Nervosa: Nosology, Diagnosis, Developmental Patterns and Power-Control Dynamics." In G. Caplan and S. Lebovici (eds.), *Adolescence: Psychosocial Perspectives*. New York: Basic Books, 1969.

Spiegel, H., and Spiegel, D. *Trance and Treatment: Clinical Uses of Hypnosis*. New York: Basic Books, 1978.

Thakur, K. S. "Treatment of Anorexia Nervosa with Hypnotherapy." In H. T. Wain (ed.), *Clinical Hypnosis in Medicine*. Chicago: Yearbook Medical Publishers, 1980.

Meir Gross is head of the Section of Eating Disorders Unit at the Cleveland Clinic Foundation in Cleveland, Ohio.

Index

Welch, G. J., 73, 85
Wells, L. A., 83
Wermuth, B. M., 99, 107
West, D. B., 58
Wetstein, L., 21n
Whyte, H. M., 48, 56
Willard, S. G., 30, 36
Williams, R. H., 50, 58
Wilmore, D. W., 22, 24, 27, 28
Winokur, A., 15, 19, 66, 69
Winstead, D. K., 30, 37
Withers, R.F.J., 49, 58
Witter, B. A., 11
Woeber, K. A., 48, 57
Wold, P. N., 66, 69
Wolf, K. M., 30, 36
Wood, K. H., 68
Woods, S. C., 52, 58
Woods, S. W., 106
Wooley, O. W., 78, 85

Wooley, S. C., 78, 85
Wright, L., 84
Wyatt, E., 10, 12

Y

Yager, J., 11, 84
Yates, A., 42, 46
Yim, G.K.W., 57
Yonace, A., 84
York, D. A., 52, 53, 56
Young, J. B., 9, 12
Younger, D., 58
Yurgelun-Todd, D., 68, 84, 106

Z

Zeigler, V. E., 81, 85
Zumoff, B., 11, 68
Zung, W.W.K., 81, 85

DATE DUE

3/2/91	SEP 2 3 1991		
DEC 10 1990	NOV 15 1991		
MAR 27 1991	NOV 15 1997		
OCT 09 1991	MAR 0 2 1998		
NOV 25 1991	MAR 1 6 1998		
6104847 3-19-92	NOV 10 1998		
DEC 1 4 1998	NOV 2 9 1999		
MAR 1 6 1993	DEC 2 0 2002		
OCT 27 1994	MAY 0 5 2006		
NOV 0 9 1994			
DEC 1 5 1995			
APR 2 3 1996			
NOV 8 0 1996			
DEC 0 9 1996			
APR 2 5 1997			
SEP 0 9 1997			